TEXTURE

TEXTURE

Exploring Simple Stitch Patterns in Knitwear

HANNAH FETTIG
with QUINCE & CO.

PHOTOGRAPHS BY WHITNEY HAYWARD

ISBN 978-0-986-10398-8

First Edition

Graphic design by Mary Joy Gumayagay

Printed in the United States by Puritan Press

Peaks Island, Maine

CONTENTS

68

76

84

92

98

INTRODUCTION

I love clean lines in design. The lines can be soft, but I like them clean. I have been designing simple, wearable knitwear almost exclusively in Stockinette stitch since the beginning of my career.

In 2010 I designed a sweater called the *Rocky Coast Cardigan*, which featured an all-over cable pattern. This was a departure for me, and knitters went crazy for it! Since this sweater's success, I have continued to design in my beloved Stockinette stitch, exploring drape in *Knitbot Essentials* and *Knitbot Linen*, then returning to more structured knits for *Knitbot Yoked* and *Home & Away: Knits for Everyday Adventures*. In *Home & Away*, I tried to include lots of helpful tips and information along with the patterns. After the book's release, I was excited to see that many knitters used it to knit their first sweaters. How great!

Meanwhile, I was still thinking about that cabled sweater. What if I did an entire collection of all-over textured knitwear? And what if I continued where the instruction in Home & Away *left off, and helped knitters take the leap from simple knit to textured stitch? What if we took that leap together?*

As the swatching and designing began, I realized it wasn't always simple to work with textured stitches where knit stitches usually would be. For some designs I was forced to depart from a preferred construction method or a preferred direction of knitting. When sizing the sweaters, my technical editor and I had to factor in pattern repeats on top of all the usual considerations. It was hard work, but the final collection of textured knits maintains my standard for clean, wearable knitwear!

Simple textured stitch patterns and cables were chosen for this book, with the hopes that it will serve both beginner and seasoned knitters well. I've also included additional content to support all knitters as they strive to knit garments that can fit into their everyday wardrobes.

I sincerely hope you find inspiration along with practical guidance in these pages!

Hannah Fettig
Kennebunk, Maine
July 2, 2016

LET'S CONNECT!

FIND a *Ravelry* coupon code, on the inside back cover of this book, good for one digital copy of *Texture*. If you aren't familiar with *Ravelry*, it's an invaluable website where the online knitting community gathers. Millions of users swap information on patterns, yarns, techniques and inspiration. You'll no doubt spend a lot of time online at

www.ravelry.com

JOIN the *Knitbot Knitters* group on *Ravelry* to connect with other knitters working on projects from the book!

www.ravelry.com/groups/knitbot-knitters

SHARE your knitting progress and finished projects on *Instagram* and tag @knitbot and @quinceandco; we'll repost some of our favorites!

www.instagram.com/knitbot
www.instagram.com/quinceandco

QUESTIONS about a pattern? Check in with the *Ravelry* group or send an e-mail to

info@knitbot.com

ERRATA for all patterns are available on our website

www.knitbot.com/errata

DELICATE TEXTURE

FABRIC PROPERTIES: Texture on a smaller scale can be beautifully delicate. Fabric knitted in lace and fingering weight yarns can have lovely drape and movement. A simple texture pattern adds weight and interest to the fabric.

GARMENTS WELL SUITED FOR: Delicate texture is perfect for shawls and shawlettes. It is also well suited for more dressed up cardigans, such as *Pretty Little Cardi* (page 12) and *Eventide Cardi* (page 20). The more delicate the knit, the more precious and special it can be—it's something about those tiny stitches! The extra fabric in the *Jennie Drop Shoulder* pullover (page 26) allows the fabric to drape, creating a wonderfully breezy garment.

YARN: You can use any lace or fingering weight yarns for these designs. Keep in mind that fiber content can affect how much drape you are getting. For example, Quince & Co. *Piper* includes 50% mohair, which offers extra drape along with shine, which makes those tiny textured stitches pop.

Breezy raglan

Open front

Textured columns

LACE WEIGHT YARN

PRETTY LITTLE CARDI

STITCH PATTERN

worked flat over 8 sts

ROW 1 (RS): Knit.

ROW 2 (WS): Purl.

ROW 3: K3, (p2, k6) repeat to last 5 sts, p2, k3.

ROW 4: P3, (k2, p6) repeat to last 5 sts, k2, p3.

worked in the rnd over 8 sts

RNDS 1 & 2: Knit.

RNDS 3 & 4: K3, (p2, k6) repeat to last 5 sts, p2, k3.

body

BEGIN AT THE BOTTOM

Using circular needle and a long-tail cast on, CO 278 (316, 354, 392) [430, 468, 506, 544] sts.

Beg with a WS row, work 11 rows in garter st.

NEXT ROW (RS): K3 (2, 1, 0)[3, 2, 1, 0], work Stitch patt to last 3 (2, 1, 0)[3, 2, 1, 0] st(s), knit to end.

Cont until body meas 14 (14, 14.25, 14.5)[14.75, 14.75, 15, 15]" / 35.5 (35.5, 36, 37)[37.5, 37.5, 38, 38] cm, ending with a WS row, noting last row worked in Stitch patt. Set aside.

sleeves

Using dpns and a long tail cast on, CO 66 (72, 78, 84)[90, 96, 102, 108] sts. Divide evenly over 3 dpns. Join for working in the rnd, being careful not to twist sts. Pm to mark beg of the rnd.

Beg with a purl rnd, work in garter st for 11 rnds.

NEXT RND: K1 (0, 3, 2)[1, 0, 3, 2], work in Stitch patt to last 1 (0, 3, 2) [1, 0, 3, 2] st(s), knit to end.

INC RND: K1, M1L, work in Stitch patt to last st, M1R, k1. 2 sts inc.

Rep this inc rnd every 12 (8, 7, 6)[5, 4, 4, 4] rnds 5 (8, 5, 6)[11, 17, 11, 2] times more, then every - (-, 6, 5)[4, -, 3, 3] rnds 0 (0, 5, 6)[3, 0, 8, 20] times more. 78 (90, 100, 110)[120, 132, 142, 154] sts.

Cont as est until sleeve meas 8.5" / 21.5 cm, ending with same rnd of Stitch patt as for body. Place first and last 3 (4, 5, 6)[7, 8, 9, 10] sts on a stitch holder. Transfer remaining 72 (82, 90, 98)[106, 116, 124, 134] sleeve sts to a stitch holder.

Break yarn, leaving a tail 8–10" / 20–25 cm long. Set aside and rep instructions for second sleeve.

yoke

JOIN BODY AND SLEEVES FOR YOKE

Return to body sts, ready to work a RS row.

NEXT ROW (RS): BO 17 (18, 19, 20)[21, 22, 23, 24] sts, work 63 (73, 83, 93)[103, 113, 123, 133] right front sts as est, slip next 6 (8, 10, 12) [14, 16, 18, 20] sts on a stitch holder for underarm, pm, work 72 (82,

finished measurements

Chest circumference: 32 (36, 40, 44)[48, 52, 56, 60]" / 81.5 (91.5, 101.5, 112)[122, 132, 142, 152.5] cm

Shown in size 36" / 91.5 cm with 2" / 5 cm of positive ease.

yarn

4 (4, 5, 6)[7, 7, 8, 9] skeins Quince & Co. *Piper* (50% Texas super kid mohair, 50% Texas superfine merino; 305 yd / 279 m per 50 g skein) in Abilene

OR 1025 (1200, 1400, 1625)[1875, 2100, 2375, 2650] yd / 925 (1100, 1300, 1500)[1700, 1925, 2175, 2425] m of lace or fingering weight yarn

needles

US 3 / 3.25 mm:

- 32" / 80 cm circular needle
- set of double-pointed needles

Or size needed to obtain gauge.

notions

Stitch markers, stitch holders or waste yarn, tapestry needle

gauge

28 sts and 44 rows = 4" / 10 cm in Stitch pattern

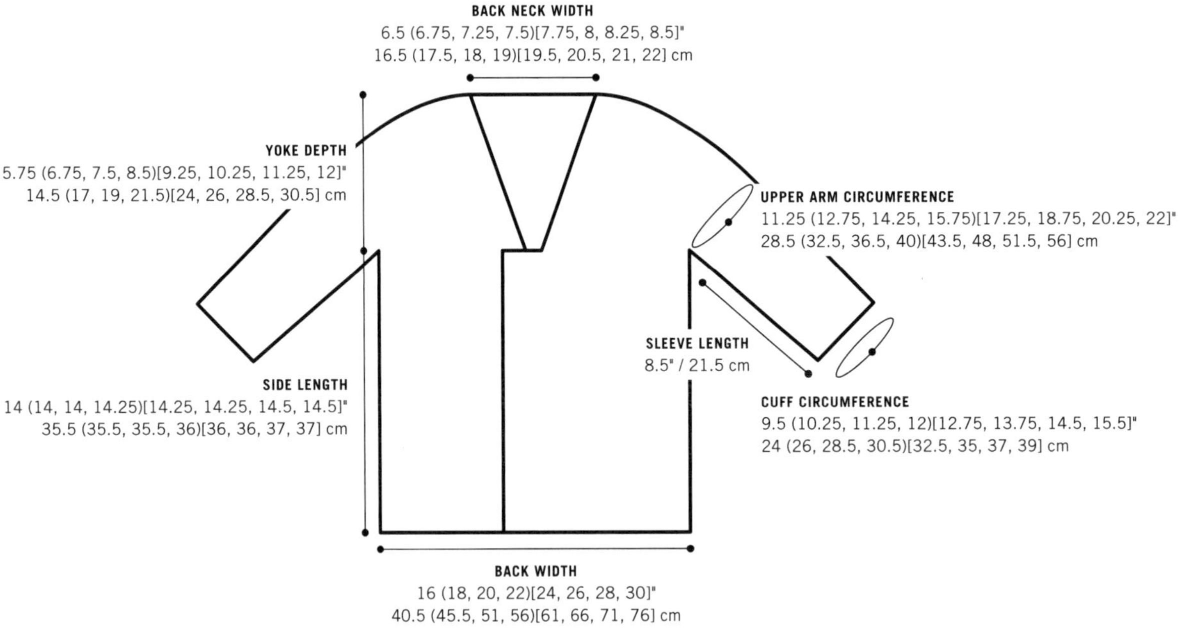

90, 98)[106, 116, 124, 134] sleeve sts as est, pm, work 106 (118, 130, 142)[154, 166, 178, 190] back sts as est, slip next 6 (8, 10, 12)[14, 16, 18, 20] sts on a stitch holder for underarm, pm, work 72 (82, 90, 98) [106, 116, 124, 134] sleeve sts as est, pm, work 80 (91, 102, 113)[124, 135, 146, 157] left front sts as est.

NEXT ROW (WS): BO 17 (18, 19, 20)[21, 22, 23, 24] sts, (work as est to 1 st before m, p1, sm, p1) 4 times, work to end. 376 (428, 476, 524) [572, 624, 672, 724] sts.

DEC ROW (RS): (K1, ssk, work as est to 3 sts before m, k2tog, k1) 5 times, slipping markers as you come to them. 10 sts dec.

Rep this dec row every RS row 29 (34, 39, 44)[49, 54, 59, 64] times more. 76 (78, 76, 74)[72, 74, 72, 74] sts: 3 front sts, 12 (12, 10, 8)[6, 6, 4, 4] sleeve sts, 46 (48, 50, 52)[54, 56, 58, 60] back sts.

BO remaining sts.

finishing

COLLAR

With circular needle and starting at the right front neck, pick up and knit 17 (18, 19, 20)[21, 22, 23, 24] sts along front BO edge, 40 (46, 53, 59)[66, 72, 78, 85] sts evenly along side neck edge, 76 (78, 76, 74)[72, 74, 72, 74] sts along BO edge, 40 (46, 53, 59)[66, 72, 78, 85] sts evenly along side neck edge, and 17 (18, 19, 20)[21, 22, 23, 24] sts along front BO edge. 190 (206, 220, 232)[246, 262, 274, 292] sts.

Work in garter st for 1" / 2.5 cm or desired length, ending with a RS row. BO all sts knitwise.

Graft both sets of underarm stitches together using Kitchener Stitch.

Weave in all ends.

Block to measurements.

FORETHOUGHT: PLANNING THE PERFECT KNIT GARMENT

Many knit because they love the journey. Keeping hands busy while in a relaxed state, being so pleasantly productive, it's a big part of why many are drawn to handwork. But what makes the journey even more satisfying is knowing that we're heading toward a desirable destination. When we're done knitting, we want to have created something that fits our body and fits into our wardrobe. Here are some practical things you can do to knit more wearable garments.

LOOK IN YOUR CLOSET. WHAT DO YOU SEE?

Let's start with what you like to wear. If there's a lot of grey in there... maybe knitting a grey sweater instead of a bright yellow one is a good choice for you. Do you usually wear pullovers or cardigans? Do you dress up or down more often?

CHOOSE THE RIGHT YARN

Once you've picked your project, you can choose your yarn. Are you going to go with the yarn suggested in the pattern, or are you hoping to take the chance to use something from your ever-growing stash? I always say: Don't use your stash out of guilt. If there's something there that's a good fit, great! If not, don't force it. If you're looking to make something that will be part of your wardrobe for a while, make a choice you'll stay happy with.

There is color to consider, but there is also fiber content. You might touch something and think, ooh that's soft. Soft is good, yes, but understand that the softer something is, the more likely it is to pill in places where there is a lot of friction, such as under the arm. If you're knitting something for comfort, then hey, soft might be a major priority! If you are knitting something for everyday wear, think about using yarn with some durability. A blend can be a good choice, such as a small amount of cashmere or fine merino blended with a durable wool. A woolen-spun yarn like Quince & Co. *Owl* is very durable, and this particular yarn boasts 50% alpaca which is known for its soft hand. You'll find two sweaters in this book designed in *Owl*, *West End Cardigan* (page 50) and *Wharf Street Pullover* (page 60), along with the *Textured Hat & Mitts* set (page 68).

Also, a word on variegated yarn. There are SO MANY gorgeous variegated yarns out there. However, variegated yarn may not be the best choice for a textured stitch pattern. The two will be fighting for attention, and their best properties may become muddled and ultimately lost. Use variegated yarn for a Stockinette stitch pattern like the ones featured in my books *Home & Away: Knits for Everyday Adventures* and *Knitbot Essentials*—a simple backdrop for the variegation of yarn to stand out against. Use solids or heathers when working the textured patterns in this book, and you'll be giving the textured stitches that you've worked long and hard to create a stage to perform on!

CONSTRUCTION METHOD

Sweaters can be put together in different ways, which affect the overall style and fit. This collection features 3 different construction methods. A raglan can offer a more relaxed (though still elegant) fit, such as the *Pretty Little Cardi* (page 12). A set-in sleeve, where the sleeve mimics the shape of the arm, offers a more tailored fit. The *Pierside Cardigan* (page 76) with a wide folded over collar keeps this tailored sweater casual. A drop shoulder such as *Jennie* on pg 26 is a very relaxed fit, though at finer gauge this pullover is quite elegant.

FIT

Choosing which size to knit is part of making something you will actually wear. It would be great if you could try the finished sweater on before you start! While you can't do that, what you can do is try on something in your closet. Take a sweater or sweatshirt that fits you the way you would like your finished garment to fit. Using the schematic included with the pattern, compare as many measurements as you can against the piece from your closet. Choose the size that is closest to the piece that you own.

SEASONAL KNITS

If you live in a place blessed with seasons, consider adding knitwear into your wardrobe for all seasons. Something like *Eventide Cardi* on page 20 can be knit in a linen or cotton yarn and worn over summer outfits.

Textured stripes

Set in sleeves

Tailored

FINGERING WEIGHT YARN

EVENTIDE CARDI

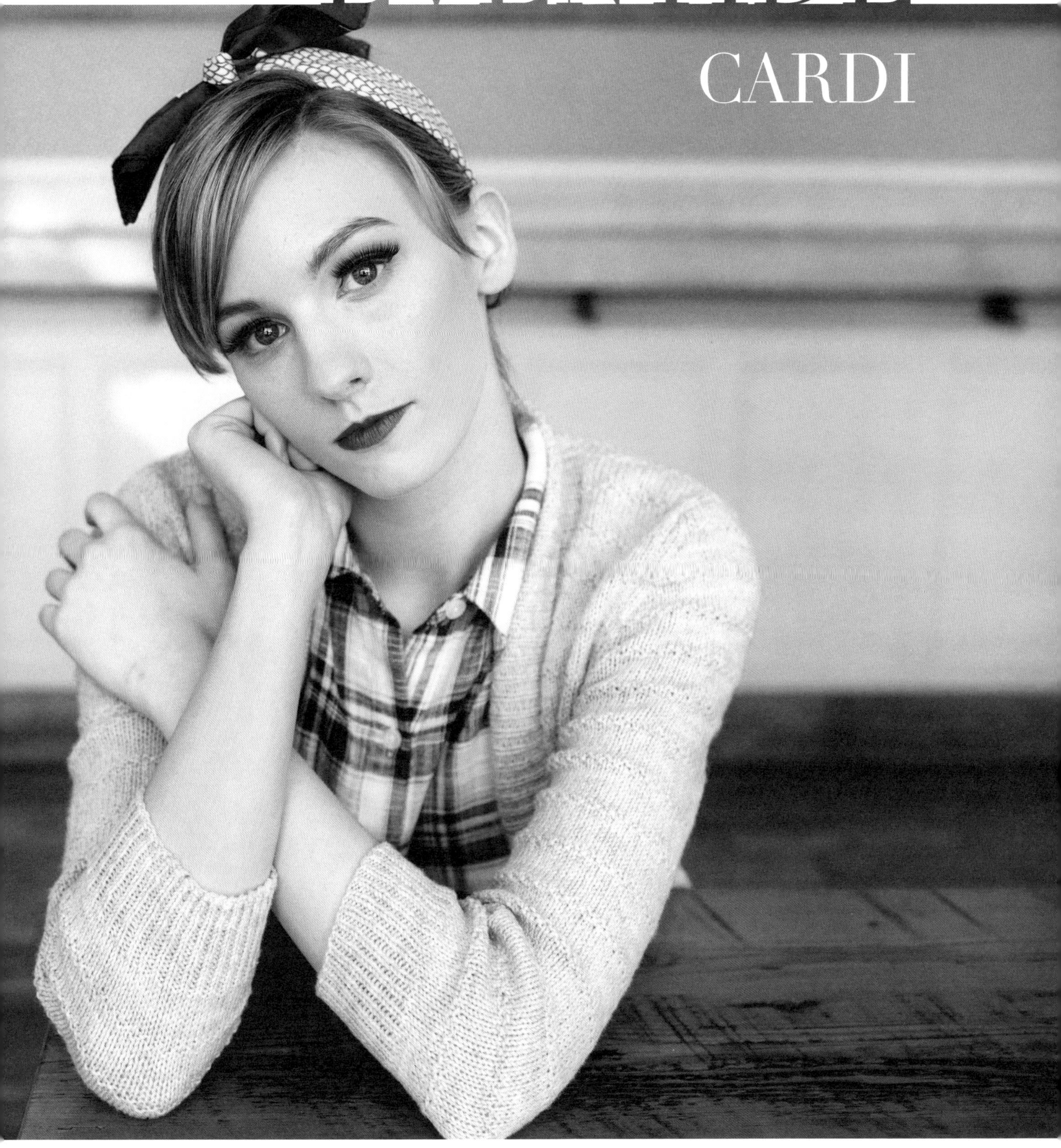

SEED STITCH STRIPE PATTERN

worked over an even number of sts

ROWS 1–8: Knit on RS, purl on WS.

ROW 9 (RS): (K1, p1) repeat to end.

ROW 10 (WS): (P1, k1) repeat to end.

worked over an odd number of sts

ROWS 1–8: Knit on RS, purl on WS.

ROW 9 (RS): (K1, p1) repeat to last st, k1.

ROW 10 (WS): (P1, k1) repeat to last st, p1.

back

BEGIN AT THE BOTTOM

Using smaller circular needle and a long-tail cast on, CO 106 (118, 130, 142, 154)[166, 178, 190, 202] sts.

RIBBING SETUP ROW (RS): K1, (k1, p1) repeat to last st, k1.

Cont in ribbing as est for 19 rows more, ending with a WS row.

Switch to larger needle.

Work Rows 1–10 of Seed Stitch Stripe patt 14 (15, 15, 16, 16)[17, 17, 18, 18] times, then work Rows 1–4 for 1 (0, 1, 0, 1)[0, 1, 0, 1] time more, ending with a WS row. Piece meas approx 16.5 (17, 17.5, 18, 18.5)[19, 19.5, 20, 20.5]" / 41.5 (43, 44, 45.5, 46.5)[48.5, 49.5, 51, 52] cm.

SHAPE ARMHOLE

BO 5 (6, 7, 8, 10)[11, 13, 14, 16] sts at beg of next 2 rows.

DEC ROW (RS): K2, ssk, work as est to last 4 sts, k2tog, k2. 2 sts dec.

Rep this dec row every RS row 1 (4, 8, 11, 14)[18, 20, 22, 24] time(s) more, then every 4 rows 4 (4, 3, 2, 1)[0, 0, 0, 0] time(s) more. 84 (88, 92, 98, 102)[106, 110, 116, 120] sts.

Cont in Seed Stitch Stripe patt until Rows 1–10 have been worked 21 (22, 23, 24, 25)[26, 27, 28, 29] times total, ending with a WS row. Armhole meas approx 6.5 (7, 7.5, 8, 8.5)[9, 9.5, 10, 10.5]" / 16.5 (18, 19, 20.5, 21.5)[23, 24, 25.5, 26.5] cm.

SHAPE SHOULDERS

BO 9 (10, 10, 11, 12)[12, 13, 14, 14] sts at beg of next 2 rows, then BO 10 (10, 11, 12, 12)[13, 13, 14, 15] sts at beg of next 2 rows. BO 46 (48, 50, 52, 54)[56, 58, 60, 62] rem back neck sts.

left front

Using smaller circular needle and a long-tail cast on, CO 30 (34, 40, 44, 50)[54, 60, 64, 70] sts.

RIBBING SETUP ROW (RS): K1, (k1, p1) repeat to last st, k1.

Cont in ribbing as est for 19 rows more, ending with a WS row.

Switch to larger needle.

Work Rows 1–10 of Seed Stitch Stripe patt 14 (15, 15, 16, 16)[17, 17, 18, 18] times, then work Rows 1–4 for 1 (0, 1, 0, 1)[0, 1, 0, 1] time

finished measurements

Chest circumference: 32.5 (36.25, 40, 43.75, 47.5) [51, 54.75, 58.5, 62.25]" / 83 (92, 101.5, 111, 120.5) [129.5, 139, 148.5, 158] cm

Shown in size 36.25" / 92 cm with 2.25" / 5.5 cm of positive ease.

yarn

7 (7, 8, 9, 10)[11, 12, 13, 14] skeins of Quince & Co. *Finch* (100% American wool; 221 yd / 202 m per 50 g skein) in Audouin

OR 1400 (1550, 1725, 1950, 2150)[2325, 2575, 2800, 3025] yd / 1275 (1425, 1575, 1775, 1950) [2125, 2350, 2550, 2750] m of fingering weight yarn

needles

US 5 / 3.75 mm:

- 24–32" / 60–80 cm circular needle

US 3 / 3.25 mm:

- 24–32" / 60–80 cm circular needle

Or size needed to obtain gauge.

notions

Tapestry needle

gauge

26 sts and 40 rows = 4" / 10 cm in Seed Stitch Stripe pattern using larger needles

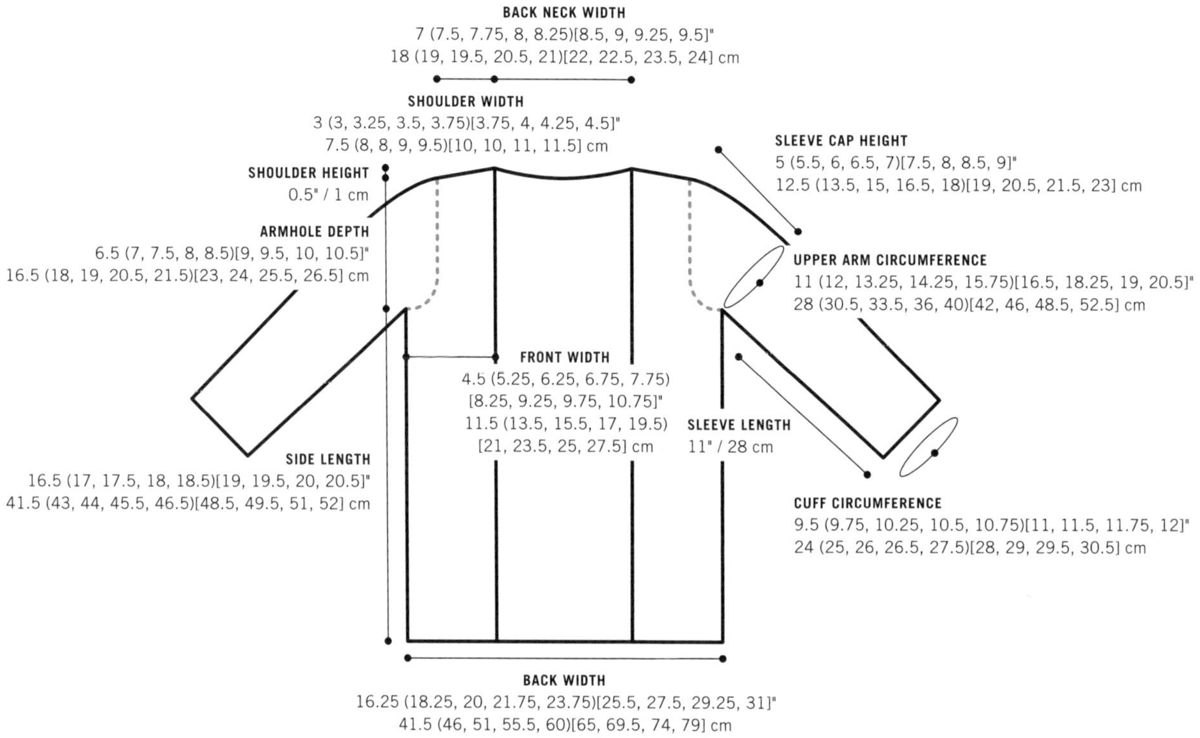

more, ending with a WS row. Piece meas approx 16.5 (17, 17.5, 18, 18.5) [19, 19.5, 20, 20.5]" / 41.5 (43, 44, 45.5, 46.5)[48.5, 49.5, 51, 52] cm.

SHAPE ARMHOLE

NEXT ROW (RS): BO 5 (6, 7, 8, 10)[11, 13, 14, 16] sts, work to end.

Work 1 WS row.

DEC ROW (RS): K2, ssk, work as est to end. 1 st dec.

Rep this dec row every RS row 1 (4, 8, 11, 14)[17, 20, 21, 24] times(s) more, then every 4 rows 4 (3, 3, 1, 1)[0, 0, 0, 0] time(s) more. 19 (20, 21, 23, 24)[25, 26, 28, 29] sts rem.

Cont in Seed Stitch Stripe patt until Rows 1–10 have been worked 21 (22, 23, 24, 25)[26, 27, 28, 29] times total, ending with a WS row. Armhole meas approx 6.5 (7, 7.5, 8, 8.5)[9, 9.5, 10, 10.5]" / 16.5 (18, 19, 20.5, 21.5)[23, 24, 25.5, 26.5] cm.

SHAPE SHOULDER

BO 9 (10, 10, 11, 12)[12, 13, 14, 14] sts, knit to end.

Purl 1 WS row.

BO remaining 10 (10, 11, 12, 12)[13, 13, 14, 15] sts.

right front

Using smaller circular needle and a long-tail cast on, CO 30 (34, 40, 44, 50)[54, 60, 64, 70] sts.

RIBBING SETUP ROW (RS): K1, (k1, p1) repeat to last st, k1.

Cont in ribbing as est for 19 rows more, ending with a WS row.

Switch to larger needle.

Work Rows 1–10 of Seed Stitch Stripe patt 14 (15, 15, 16, 16)[17, 17, 18, 18] times, then work Row 1 once more.

SIZES 32.5 (-, 40, -, 47.5)[-, 54.75, -, 62.75]" / 83 (-, 101.5, -, 120.5)[-, 139, -, 158] CM ONLY

Work Rows 2–5 once more.

ALL SIZES

SHAPE ARMHOLE

NEXT ROW (WS): BO 5 (6, 7, 8, 10)[11, 13, 14, 16] sts, work to end.

DEC ROW (RS): Work as est to last 4 sts, k2tog, k2. 1 st dec.

Rep this dec row every RS row 1 (4, 8, 11, 14)[17, 20, 21, 24] time(s) more, then every 4 rows 4 (3, 3, 1, 1)[0, 0, 0, 0] time(s) more. 19 (20, 21, 23, 24)[25, 26, 28, 29] sts rem.

Cont in Seed Stitch Stripe patt until Rows 1–10 have been worked 21 (22, 23, 24, 25)[26, 27, 28, 29] times total, then work Row 1 once more, ending with a RS row. Armhole meas approx 6.5 (7, 7.5, 8, 8.5)[9, 9.5, 10, 10.5]" / 16.5 (18, 19, 20.5, 21.5)[23, 24, 25.5, 26.5] cm.

SHAPE SHOULDER

NEXT ROW (WS): BO 9 (10, 10, 11, 12)[12, 13, 14, 14] sts, purl to end.

Knit 1 RS row.

BO remaining 10 (10, 11, 12, 12)[13, 13, 14, 15] sts.

sleeves

Using smaller circular needle and a long-tail cast on, CO 62 (64, 66, 68, 70)[72, 74, 76, 78] sts.

RIBBING SETUP ROW (RS): K1, (k1, p1) repeat to last st, k1.

Cont in ribbing as est for 19 rows, ending with a WS row.

Switch to larger needle.

INC ROW (RS): K2, M1L, work in Seed Stitch Stripe patt to last 2 sts, M1R, k2. 2 sts inc.

Rep this inc row every 10 (10, 10, 8, 6)[4, 4, 2, 2] rows 4 (6, 9, 10, 15) [6, 18, 1, 9] time(s) more, then every - (-, -, 10, -)[6, 6, 4, 4] rows 0 (0, 0, 1, 0)[11, 3, 22, 18] time(s) more. 72 (78, 86, 92, 102)[108, 118, 124, 134] sts.

Cont in Seed Stitch Stripe patt until Rows 1–10 have been worked 9 times total, ending with a WS row. Sleeve meas approx 11" / 28 cm.

SHAPE CAP

BO 5 (6, 7, 8, 10)[11, 13, 14, 16] sts at beg of next 2 rows.

DEC ROW (RS): K2, ssk, work as est to last 4 sts, k2tog, k2. 2 sts dec.

Rep this dec row every RS row 6 (7, 9, 10, 11)[12, 14, 15, 16] times more, then every 4 rows 4 times more, then every RS row 7 (8, 9, 10, 12)[13, 14, 15, 17] times more. 26 sts.

Work 1 WS row.

BO 2 sts at beg of next 2 rows, then BO 3 sts at beg of next 2 rows.

BO remaining 16 sts.

finishing

Sew shoulder seams.

COLLAR

Using smaller circular needle and beg at the bottom right edge, pick up and knit 2 sts for every 3 rows up the right front of the cardigan, pick up and knit 46 (48, 50, 52, 54)[56, 58, 60, 62] sts evenly across back neck, then pick up and knit 2 sts for every 3 rows down the left front. Adjust, if needed, so there is an odd number of sts.

RIBBING SETUP ROW (WS): (K1, p1) repeat to last st, k1.

Cont in ribbing as est for 4" / 10 cm.

Switch to larger circular needle.

BO loosely in ribbing.

Sew sleeve cap into armhole. Sew sleeve and side seams using Mattress Stitch.

Weave in all ends. Block to measurements.

Location: Eventide Oyster Company, Portland, Maine

Drop shoulder

Easy fit

Drape

FINGERING WEIGHT YARN

DROP SHOULDER

BROKEN RIB PATTERN

worked in the rnd over an even number of sts

RND 1: Knit.

RND 2: (K1, p1) repeat to end.

RND 3: Knit.

RND 4: (P1, k1) repeat to end.

worked flat over an even number of sts

ROW 1 (RS): Knit.

ROW 2 (WS): (K1, p1) repeat to end.

ROW 3: Knit.

ROW 4: (P1, k1) repeat to end.

body

BEGIN AT THE BOTTOM

Using smaller circular needle and a long-tail cast on, CO 228 (252, 276, 300, 324)[348, 372, 396, 420] sts. Join for working in the rnd, being careful not to twist sts. Pm to mark beg of the rnd.

RIBBING SETUP RND: (K1, p1) repeat to end.

Cont in ribbing as est for 17 rnds more.

Switch to larger needles.

Begin working in Broken Rib patt. Cont until piece meas 15.5 (16, 16.5, 17, 17.5)[18, 18.5, 19, 19.5]" / 39.5 (40.5, 42, 43, 44.5)[45.5, 47, 48.5, 49.5] cm, ending with Row 1 or 3 of Broken Rib patt.

Work 114 (126, 138, 150, 162)[174, 186, 198, 210] sts, turn. Place remaining sts on a stitch holder to be worked later, noting last row worked in Broken Rib patt. Piece will now be worked back and forth.

back

SIZES - (-, 46, 50, 54)[58, 62, 66, 70]" / - (-, 117, 127, 137)[147.5, 157.5, 167.5, 178] CM ONLY

BO - (-, 3, 6, 9)[12, 15, 18, 21] sts at beg of next 2 rows. - (-, 132, 138, 144)[150, 156, 162, 168] sts.

ALL SIZES

NEXT ROW (WS): P1, work as est to last st, p1.

NEXT ROW (RS): K1, work as est to last st, k1.

Cont as est for 5 (7, 9, 9, 11)[11, 13, 13, 15] rows more, ending with a WS row.

SHOULDER INC ROW (RS): K1, M1L, work to last st, M1R, k1. 2 sts inc.

Rep this inc row every 8 (10, 12, 12, 14)[14, 16, 16, 18] rows 4 times more. 124 (136, 142, 148, 154)[160, 166, 172, 178] sts.

Cont as est until armhole meas 6 (6.5, 7, 7.5, 8)[8.5, 9, 9.5, 10]" / 15 (16.5, 18, 19, 20.5)[21.5, 23, 24, 25.5] cm, ending with a WS row.

finished measurements

Chest circumference: 38 (42, 46, 50, 54)[58, 62, 66, 70]" / 96.5 (106.5, 117, 127, 137) [147.5, 157.5, 167.5, 178] cm

Shown in size 38" / 96.5 cm with 4" / 10 cm of positive ease.

yarn

7 (8, 9, 10, 11)[12, 13, 14, 15] skeins Quince & Co. *Tern* (75% American wool, 25% silk; 221 yd / 202 m per 50 g skein) in Beach Glass

OR 1475 (1675, 1875, 2100, 2325)[2550, 2800, 3050, 3325] yd / 1350 (1525, 1725, 1900, 2125) [2325, 2550, 2800, 3025] m of fingering weight yarn

needles

US 5 / 3.75 mm:

- 24–32" / 60–80 cm circular needle
- set of double-pointed needles

US 3 / 3.25 mm:

- 24–32" / 60–80 cm circular needle
- set of double-pointed needles

Or size needed to obtain gauge.

notions

Stitch markers, stitch holders or waste yarn, tapestry needle

gauge

24 sts and 36 rnds = 4" / 10 cm in Broken Rib pattern using larger needles

BEGIN SHOULDER SHAPING

BO 14 (15, 16, 17, 17)[18, 19, 19, 20] sts at beg of next 6 (2, 4, 6, 2)[4, 6, 2, 4] rows, then BO - (16, 17, -, 18)[19, -, 20, 21] sts at beg of next 0 (4, 2, 0, 4)[2, 0, 4, 2] rows.

BO 40 (42, 44, 46, 48)[50, 52, 54, 56] rem back neck sts.

front

Place 114 (126, 138, 150, 162)[174, 186, 198, 210] held sts back on needles, ready to work a RS row.

SIZES - (-, 46, 50, 54)[58, 62, 66, 70]" / - (-, 117, 127, 137)[147.5, 157.5, 167.5, 178] CM ONLY

BO - (-, 3, 6, 9)[12, 15, 18, 21] sts at beg of next 2 rows. - (-, 132, 138, 144)[150, 156, 162, 168] sts.

ALL SIZES

NEXT ROW (RS): K1, work as est to last st, k1.

NEXT ROW (WS): P1, work as est to last st, p1.

Cont as est for 6 (8, 10, 10, 12)[12, 14, 14, 16] more rows, ending with a WS row.

INC ROW (RS): K1, M1L, work as est to last st, M1R, k1. 2 sts inc.

Rep this inc row every 8 (10, 12, 12, 14)[14, 16, 16, 18] rows 4 times more.

AT THE SAME TIME, when armhole meas 3 (3.5, 4, 4, 4.25)[4.25, 4.75, 4.75, 5.25]" / 7.5 (8.5, 10, 10, 11)[11, 12, 12, 13.5] cm, shape neck as follows:

On next RS row, BO center 18 (20, 20, 22, 22)[24, 24, 26, 26] sts, work to end as est.

Place left shoulder sts on a stitch holder, noting last row worked in Broken Rib patt.

RIGHT SHOULDER

Work 1 WS row.

NECK DEC ROW (RS): K1, ssk, work to end. 1 st dec.

Rep this neck dec row every RS row 10 (10, 11, 11, 12)[12, 13, 13, 14] times more. 40 (42, 44, 46, 48)[50, 52, 54, 56] sts once neck and armhole shaping are complete.

Cont as est until armhole meas 6 (6.5, 7, 7.5, 8)[8.5, 9, 9.5, 10]" / 15 (16.5, 18, 19, 20.5)[21.5, 23, 24, 25.5] cm, ending with a RS row.

BEGIN SHOULDER SHAPING

BO 14 (15, 16, 17, 17)[18, 19, 19, 20] sts at beg of the next 3 (1, 2, 3, 1)[2, 3, 1, 2] WS row(s).

BO - (16, 17, -, 18)[19, -, 20, 21] sts at beg of the next 0 (2, 1, 0, 2)[1, 0, 2, 1] WS row(s).

LEFT SHOULDER

Place held left shoulder sts back on needles, ready to work a WS row.

Work 1 WS row.

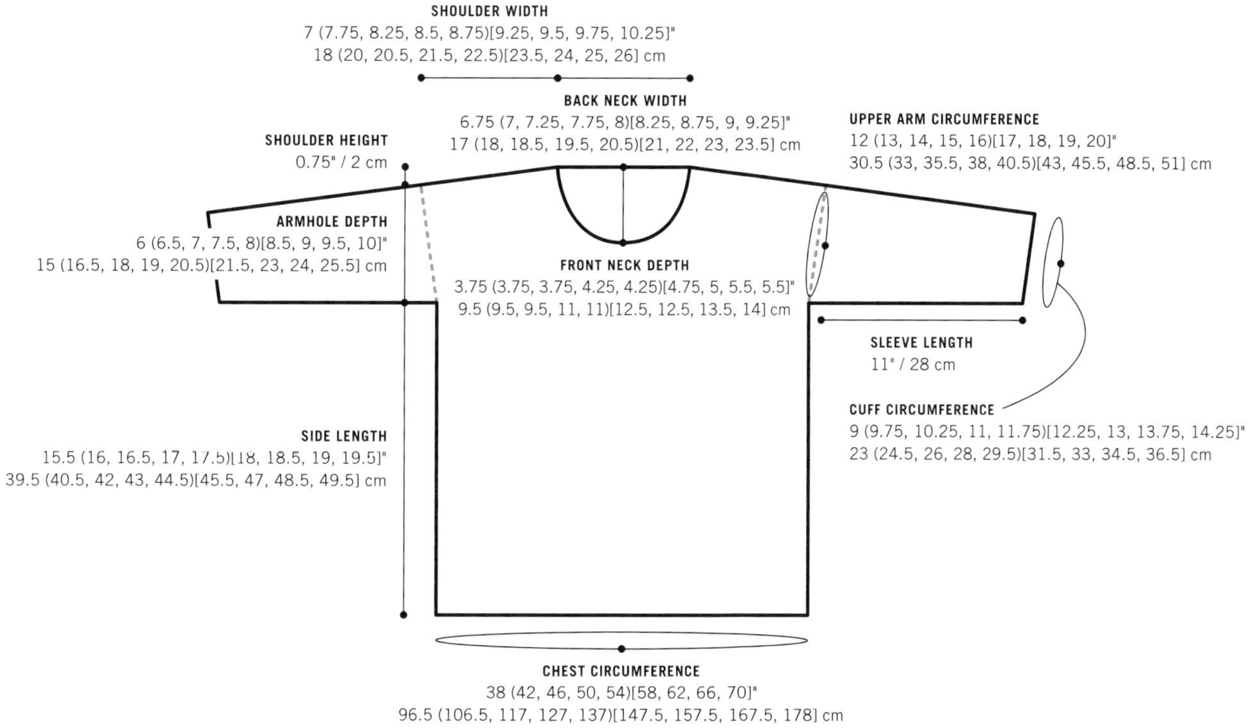

NECK DEC ROW (RS): Work to last 3 sts, k2tog, k1. 1 st dec.

Rep this neck dec row every RS row 10 (10, 11, 11, 12)[12, 13, 13, 14] times more. 40 (42, 44, 46, 48)[50, 52, 54, 56] sts once neck and armhole shaping are complete.

Cont as est until armhole meas 6 (6.5, 7, 7.5, 8)[8.5, 9, 9.5, 10]" / 15 (16.5, 18, 19, 20.5)[21.5, 23, 24, 25.5] cm, ending with a WS row.

BEGIN SHOULDER SHAPING

BO 14 (15, 16, 17, 17)[18, 19, 19, 20] sts at beg of next 3 (1, 2, 3, 1) [2, 3, 1, 2] RS row(s).

BO - (16, 17, -, 18)[19, -, 20, 21] sts at beg of next 0 (2, 1, 0, 2)[1, 0, 2, 1] RS row(s).

Sew shoulder seams.

sleeves

Using larger dpns, RS facing and beg at the center of the underarm, pick up and knit 72 (78, 84, 90, 96)[102, 108, 114, 120] sts evenly around armhole edge. Join for working in the rnd. Pm to mark beg of the rnd.

Work in Broken Rib patt for 8 (7, 7, 6, 6)[5, 5, 5, 5] rnds.

DEC RND: Ssk, work as est to last 2 sts, k2tog. 2 sts dec.

Rep this dec rnd every 8 (7, 7, 6, 6)[5, 5, 5, 5] rnds 6 (9, 3, 9, 4)[13, 9, 5, 1] time(s) more, then every 7 (-, 6, 5, 5)[-, 4, 4, 4] rnds 2 (0, 7, 2, 8) [0, 5, 10, 15] times more. 54 (58, 62, 66, 70)[74, 78, 82, 86] sts.

Cont as est until sleeve meas 9" / 23 cm, or 2" / 5 cm shorter than desired length.

Switch to smaller dpns.

RIBBING SETUP RND: (K1, p1) repeat to end.

Cont in ribbing as est for 17 rnds more.

BO loosely in ribbing.

finishing

NECKBAND

Using smaller circ, pick up and knit an even number of sts around neck edge. Pm to mark beg of the rnd.

RIBBING SETUP RND: (K1, p1) repeat to end.

Cont in ribbing as est for 13 rnds more.

BO loosely in ribbing.

Weave in all ends.

Block to measurements.

WORKING IN STITCH PATTERN

KNIT AND PURL

If you've worked in Stockinette stitch, then you know how to knit and purl. Now we're going to play with alternating knit and purl stitches to create textured stitch patterns! At first it may feel like slow going, but don't be discouraged. You were probably slow at Stockinette stitch when you first learned to knit, but you got faster. The same will happen with texture.

When knitting Stockinette, you knit an entire row with your yarn at the back. Then on the WS you purl a row with your yarn in the front. When alternating knit and purl stitches, you'll need to keep switching your yarn from back to front.

Step 1 *(a, b)*: Knit, yarn in back.
Step 2 *(c, d)*: Purl, yarn in front.

See page 48 on how to read your knitting if you lose track of whether you should be working a knit or purl stitch next!

CABLE

A cable is created by crossing stitches in front of or behind each other.

C4B

This cable is worked over 4 stitches and leans to the right.

Step 1 *(e)*: Slip 2 sts onto a cable needle (cn) and hold in back of your work.
Step 2 *(f)*: Knit 2 sts.
Step 3 *(g, h)*: Knit 2 sts from cn.

C4F

This cable is worked over 4 stitches and leans to the left.

Step 1 *(i)*: Slip 2 sts onto a cn and hold it in front of your work.
Step 2 *(j)*: Knit 2 sts.
Step 3 *(k, l)*: Knit 2 sts from cn.

MEASURING GAUGE IN TEXTURED STITCH PATTERN

If your finished knits never seem to come out the right size, chances are you've been skipping the all-important step of "getting gauge". If that's the case, no judgment, you are certainly not alone! But if you'd like to experience the joy of knitting a predictable garment, I hope this section can help you.

WHAT IS GAUGE?

Gauge is the number of stitches and rows (or rounds if knitting in the round) achieved over 1" / 2.5 cm of knitted fabric. It is often stated over 4" / 10 cm. Measuring the gauge of a textured stitch pattern can be a bit trickier than measuring Stockinette stitch gauge. That's because Stockinette stitch is easier to "read". We'll talk more about reading your knitting on page 48. For now, let's talk about how to knit a good swatch.

HOW TO KNIT YOUR SWATCH

After years of knitting tiny swatches, sometimes leaving them on the needles and squeezing my ruler onto the tiny bit of fabric attached, I finally gave in to knitting large swatches. What once felt like a waste of time became an invaluable exercise that led me to knit sweaters and accessories that came out the intended size! As stated above, most often gauge is listed over 4" / 10 cm. So here's what we need to do: knit a swatch bigger than that. Pam Allen taught me to knit a 6" / 15 cm swatch, and she is right, it's the best size. Let's say we are going to cast on a gauge swatch for the *Eventide Cardi* (page 20). The target gauge is 26 sts and 40 rows over 4" / 10 cm. This breaks down to 6.5 sts and 10 rows per 1" / 2.5 cm.

With our US 5 needle, which is the stated gauge needle, we are going to cast on 39 sts (6.5 sts times 6).

Then we work in the stitch pattern for 60 rows total (10 rows times 6) then bind off all stitches.

Now we'll wet block our swatch. That means soak it in some soapy water and let it dry flat, being gentle with those textured stitches. We don't want to squish them flat!

HOW TO MEASURE YOUR SWATCH

Take your nice square swatch and lay it on a flat surface. Using a 4" / 10 cm gauge square (such as the one shown from Twig & Horn) or a stiff ruler, take a measurement in a few different areas of your swatch. If you're getting more stitches over 4" / 10 cm than stated, it means you need to go up a needle size. If you're getting fewer stitches over 4" / 10 cm than stated, you need to go down a needle size. And though this may come as terrible news, you do need to cast on a new gauge swatch to verify the results. It may feel painful, but know that by carrying out this important step you are ensuring that your garment will come out the correct size. We all want that, right? Think of all the knitting you're about to do on this garment!

HOW TO MEASURE CABLES

Cables can be a bit trickier to measure, as they can vary in width at different points. See page 48 for tips on reading cables, which will help you immensely if you lose your place while working cables. To check our gauge, let's cast on a few cable repeats worth of stitches.

For example, let's swatch for the *Pierside Cardigan*, an all-over horseshoe cable cardigan (page 76). The target gauge is 26 sts and 32 rows over 4" / 10 cm. That's 6.5 sts and 8 rows per 1" / 2.5 cm. The cables are 16 sts wide, so let's cast on 48 sts, which means we'll be working 3 cable repeats. Then we'll repeat rows 1–8 of the cable pattern 6 times, which is 6 times 8 for a total of 48 rows.

Once we've blocked our swatch we can measure for gauge. For this we'll do a little math: measure one full pattern repeat, for width measuring at the widest point. One 16-stitch cable, at 6.5 sts per inch, should measure 2.25" / 6 cm wide and 1" / 2.5 cm tall. If it's smaller, you need to go up a needle size. If it's larger, you need to go down a needle size.

SWATCHING FOR FABRIC

Another thing you can do with your gauge swatch is hold it up and observe how the fabric behaves. Are you happy with the drape, the fiber, the color? If your heart is telling you this isn't quite what you had in mind, save yourself the time of knitting an entire garment in this fabric, only to feel the same way! That's the beauty of swatching: you can take the chance to try out different yarn options.

FINALLY...

Hey, don't throw those swatches out! These can be excellent tools to practice seaming and picking up stitches, which we'll talk about later in this book.

twig & horn
metric
american

Simple

Graceful

Versatile

FINGERING WEIGHT YARN

SUPERMOON KERCHIEF

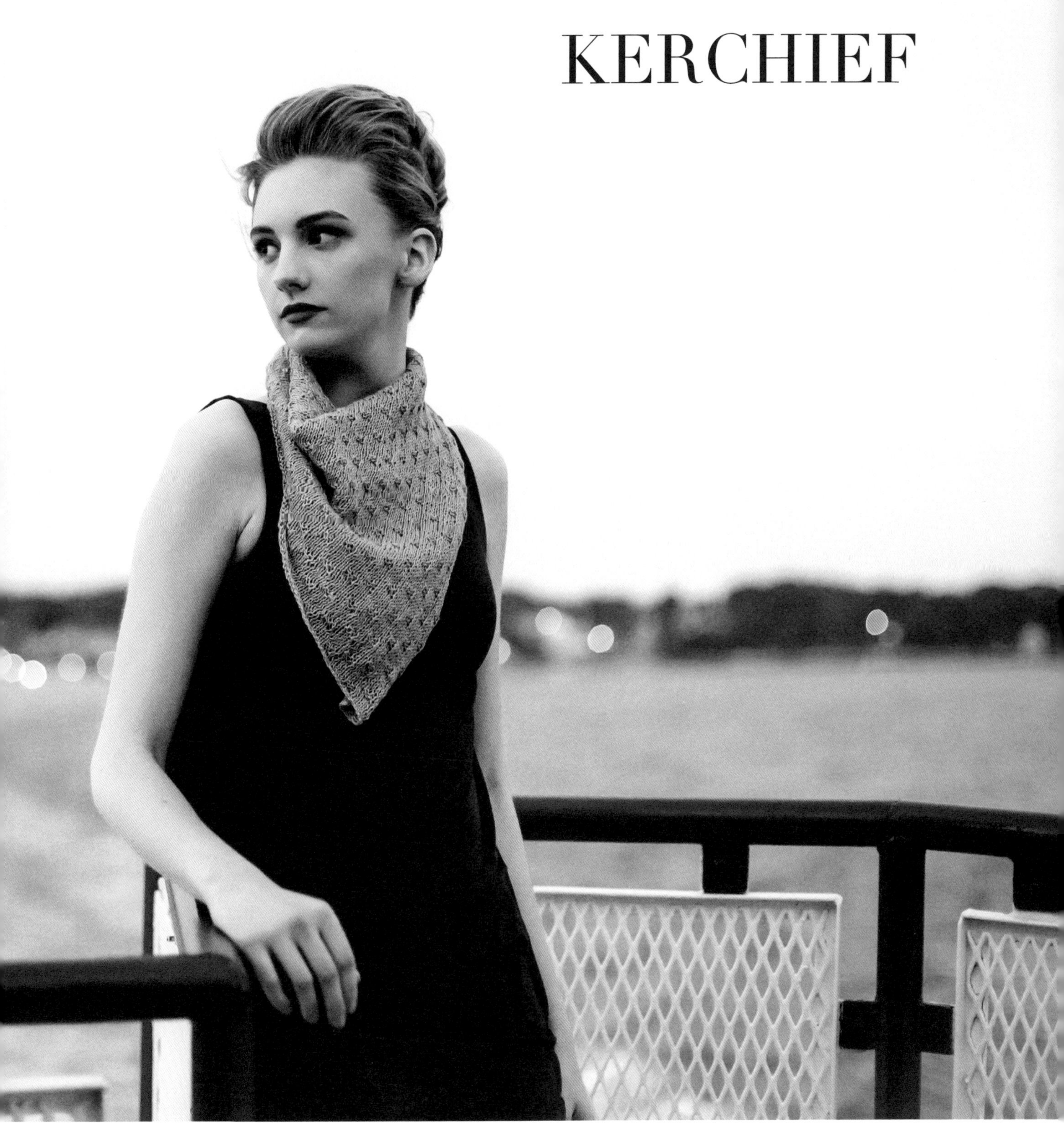

kerchief

Using a long-tail cast on, CO 128 sts.

BEGIN STITCH PATTERN

ROW 1 (RS): Knit.

ROW 2 (WS): Purl.

ROW 3: (P2, k6) repeat to end.

ROW 4: (P6, k2) repeat to end.

ROW 5: Knit.

ROW 6: Purl.

ROW 7: K4, (p2, k6) repeat to last 4 sts, p2, k2.

ROW 8: P2, (k2, p6) repeat to last 6 sts, k2, p4.

Rep these 8 rows until kerchief meas 21" / 53.5 cm, ending with Row 1 or 5 of Stitch patt.

BO all sts purlwise.

finishing

Weave in all ends. Block to measurements.

finished measurements

21" / 53.5 cm square

yarn

3 skeins Quince & Co. *Sparrow* (100% Organic linen; 168 yd / 155 m per 50 g skein) in Sans

OR 500 yd / 450 m of fingering weight linen yarn

needles

US 4 / 3.5 mm:

- 24" / 40 cm circular needle

Or size needed to obtain gauge.

notions

Tapestry needle

gauge

24 sts and 30 rows = 4" / 10 cm in Stitch pattern

EVERYDAY TEXTURE

FABRIC PROPERTIES: Most of my "everyday knits", the ones I grab the most frequently, are between a dk / sport weight and worsted weight. Adding simple texture in these weights adds interest, while still providing a comfortable lightweight fabric. Some more complex stitch patterns, especially cables, may make the fabric so dense that it bumps it into the BIG TEXTURE category, like the *Pierside Cardigan* (page 76). The garments in this chapter were designed to be lightweight enough to be appropriate for everyday wear. You can still achieve drape in texture at this weight, though it's not the first property that comes to mind.

GARMENTS WELL SUITED FOR: I am almost always a cardigan girl. However, in my playing with textured stitches, especially in a medium weight, I found myself thinking of pullovers. You'll find a unisex pullover in moss stitch on page 42 which is comfortable to wear. This wardrobe staple could be worn fitted or oversized. Cables are introduced in this section, with two sweaters knitted in Quince & Co. *Owl*. One cable is used for a collar in an otherwise moss stitch covered cardigan on page 50. A classic all-over honeycomb stitch pullover can be found on page 60.

YARN: Depending on which yarn you choose the fabric can feel more or less textured. Using a smooth, round yarn like Quince & Co. *Lark* will create smooth, clearly defined texture (see *Boatyard Pullover*, page 42) while using a woolen-spun yarn like Quince & Co. *Owl* adds additional character and depth with each textured stitch.

Unisex sizing

Classic pullover

Top down raglan

WORSTED WEIGHT YARN

BOATYARD PULLOVER

MOSS STITCH PATTERN

worked flat over an odd number of sts

ROW 1 (RS): (K1, p1) repeat to last st, k1.
ROW 2 (WS): (P1, k1) repeat to last st, p1.
ROW 3: (P1, k1) repeat to last st, p1.
ROW 4: (K1, p1) repeat to last st, k1.

worked in the rnd over an even number of sts

RNDS 1 & 2: (K1, p1) repeat to end.
RNDS 3 & 4: (P1, k1) repeat to end.

yoke

BEGIN AT THE TOP

Using larger circular needle and a long-tail cast on, CO 53 (55, 57, 59, 61)[63, 65, 67, 69] sts.

SETUP ROW (WS): P3, pm, p7, pm, p33 (35, 37, 39, 41)[43, 45, 47, 49], pm, p7, pm, p3.

ESTABLISH STITCH PATTERN

NOTE: Moss Stitch pattern on Left Front is shifted by one row so that pattern lines up seamlessly when work is joined in the round.

ROW 1 (RS): K1, p1, k1, sm, * k1, (k1, p1) to 2 sts before m, k2, sm; rep from * twice more, k3.

ROW 2 (WS): P3, sm, * p1, (p1, k1) to 2 sts before m, p2, sm; rep from * twice more, p3.

ESTABLISH RAGLAN AND NECK INCREASES

ROW 1—INC ROW (RS): K1, M1L, k1, M1R, k1, sm, * k1, M1L, p1, (k1, p1) to 1 st before m, M1R, k1, sm; rep from * twice more, k1, M1L, p1, M1R, k1. 10 sts inc.
ROW 2 (WS): P2, k1, p2, sm, * p2, (k1, p1) to 1 st before marker, p1, sm; rep from * twice more, p2, k1, p2.
ROW 3—INC ROW (RS): K1, M1L, (k1, p1) to 2 sts before m, k1, M1R, k1, sm, * k1, M1L, p1, (k1, p1) to 1 st before m, M1R, k1; rep from * 3 times more, slipping markers as you come to them. 10 sts inc.
ROW 4: * P2, (k1, p1) to 1 st before m, p1; rep from * 4 times more, slipping markers as you come to them.

Rep Rows 3 & 4 for 3 times more. 103 (105, 107, 109, 111)[113, 115, 117, 119] sts: 13 front sts, 17 sleeve sts, 43 (45, 47, 49, 51)[53, 55, 57, 59] back sts.

NEXT ROW (RS): K1, (k1, p1) to 2 sts before m, k2, sm, * k1, M1L, p1, (k1, p1) to 1 st before m, M1R, k1, sm; rep from * twice more, k1, M1L, (p1, k1) to end, using a backward loop cast on, CO 17 (19, 21, 23, 25)[27, 29, 31, 33] sts, join for working in the rnd, (k1, p1) to 1 st before m, M1R, k1, pm for beg of rnd. 128 (132, 136, 140, 144)[148, 152, 156, 160] sts: 19 sleeve sts, 45 (47, 49, 51, 53)[55, 57, 59, 61] front and back sts.

Work 1 rnd even.

finished measurements

Chest circumference: 37.25 (41, 44.5, 48, 51.5)[55, 58.75, 62.25, 65.75]" / 95 (104, 113, 122, 131)[140, 149, 158, 167] cm

Shown in size 44.5" / 113 cm with 4.5" / 11.5 cm of positive ease.

yarn

8 (9, 10, 11, 12)[13, 14, 15, 16] skeins Quince & Co. *Lark* (100% American wool; 134 yd / 123 m per 50 g skein) in Chanterelle

OR 1025 (1150, 1275, 1400, 1550)[1675, 1825, 1950, 2125] yd / 950 (1050, 1175, 1275, 1400)[1525, 1675, 1800, 1960] m of worsted weight yarn

needles

US 8 / 5 mm:

- 32" / 80 cm circular needle
- set of double-pointed needles

US 6 / 4 mm:

- 32" / 80 cm circular needle
- set of double-pointed needles

Or size needed to obtain gauge.

notions

Stitch markers, stitch holders or waste yarn, tapestry needle

gauge

18 sts and 26 rnds = 4" / 10 cm in Moss Stitch pattern using larger needles

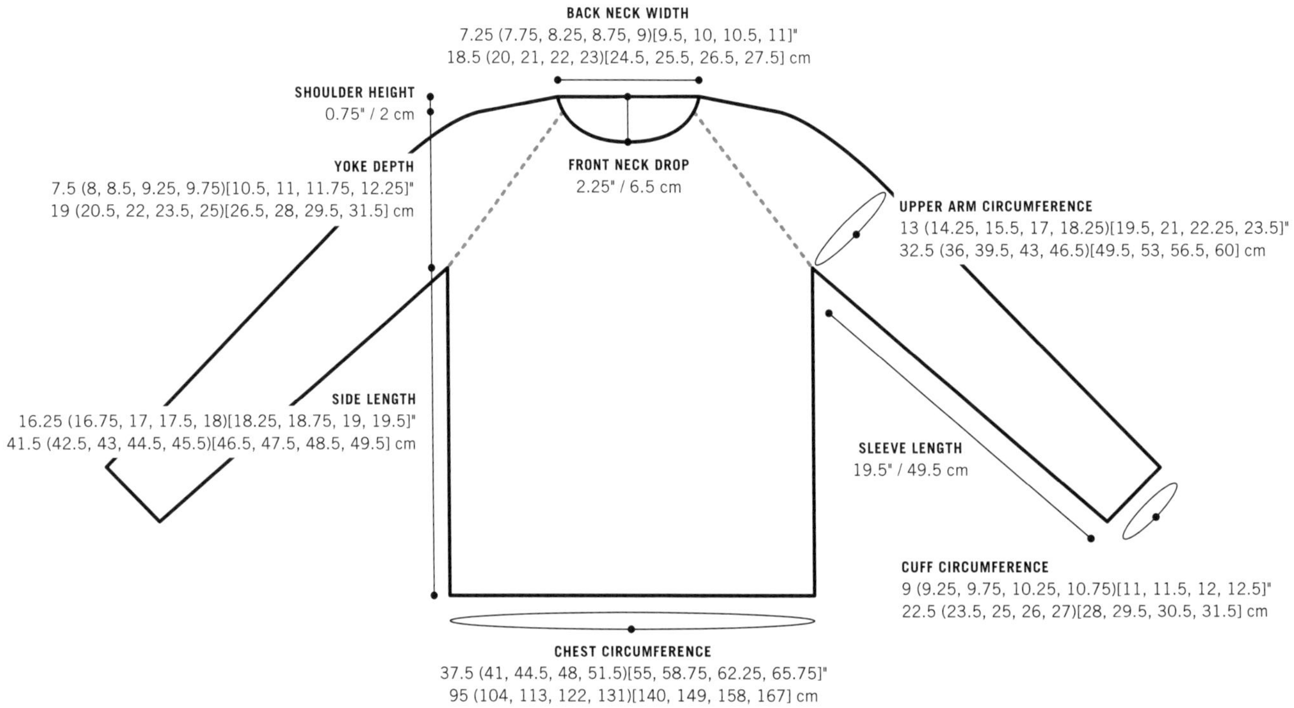

INC RND: * K1, M1L, p1, (k1, p1) to 1 st before m, M1R, k1; rep from * 3 times more, slipping markers as you come to them. 8 sts inc.

Rep this inc rnd EOR 15 (17, 19, 21, 23)[25, 27, 29, 31] times more. 256 (276, 296, 316, 336)[356, 376, 396, 416] sts: 51 (55, 59, 63, 67) [71, 75, 79, 83] sleeve sts, 77 (83, 89, 95, 101)[107, 113, 119, 125] front and back sts.

Work 3 rnds even in Moss St as est. Yoke meas approx 7.5 (8, 8.5, 9.25, 9.75)[10.5, 11, 11.75, 12.25]" / 19 (20.5, 22, 23.5, 25)[26.5, 28, 29.5, 31.5] cm.

DIVIDE SLEEVES FROM BODY

NEXT RND: * Place 51 (55, 59, 63, 67)[71, 75, 79, 83] sleeve sts on a stitch holder, using a backward loop cast on, CO 7 (9, 11, 13, 15)[17, 19, 21, 23] sts for underarm, work 77 (83, 89, 95, 101)[107, 113, 119, 125] sts as est; rep from * once more. 168 (184, 200, 216, 232)[248, 264, 280, 296] sts.

Cont as est until body meas 13.25 (13.75, 14, 14.5, 15)[15.25, 15.75, 16, 16.5]" / 33.5 (35, 35.5, 37, 38)[38.5, 40, 40.5, 42] cm from underarm, or 3" / 7.5 cm shorter than desired length.

Switch to smaller circular needle.

RIBBING SETUP RND: (K1, p1) repeat to end.

Cont in ribbing as est for 3" / 7.5 cm.

BO loosely in patt.

sleeves

Divide 51 (55, 59, 63, 67)[71, 75, 79, 83] held sleeve sts evenly over 3 larger dpns. With a 4th dpn, pick up and knit 3 (4, 5, 6, 7)[8, 9, 10, 11] sts along underarm edge, pm, pick up and knit 4 (5, 6, 7, 8)[9, 10, 11, 12] sts along underarm edge, join for working in the rnd. 58 (64, 70, 76, 82)[88, 94, 100, 106] sts.

Work in Moss St as est for 11 (9, 7, 6, 5)[5, 4, 4, 4] rnds.

DEC RND: Ssk, work to last 2 sts, k2tog. 2 sts dec.

Rep this dec rnd every 12 (10, 8, 7, 6)[6, 5, 5, 5] rnds 1 (1, 9, 10, 15) [5, 16, 8, 24] time(s) more, then every 11 (9, 7, 6, 5)[5, 4, 4, -] rnds 7 (9, 3, 4, 1)[13, 4, 14, 0] time(s) more. 40 (42, 44, 46, 48)[50, 52, 54, 56] sts.

Cont as est until sleeve meas 16.5" / 42 cm from underarm, or 3" / 7.5 cm shorter than desired length.

Switch to smaller dpns.

RIBBING SETUP RND: (K1, p1) repeat to end.

Cont in ribbing as est for 3" / 7.5 cm.

BO loosely in ribbing.

finishing

NECKBAND

Using smaller circular needle, pick up and knit 53 (55, 57, 59, 61)[63, 65, 67, 69] sts along initial CO edge, 8 sts along right side neck, 17 (19, 21, 23, 25)[27, 29, 31, 33] sts along front neck CO sts, and 8 sts along left side neck. Pm for beg of rnd. 86 (90, 94, 98, 102)[106, 110, 114, 118] sts.

RIBBING SETUP RND: (K1, p1) repeat to end.

Cont in ribbing as est for 1.5" / 4 cm.

BO loosely in ribbing.

Weave in all ends. Block to measurements.

READING YOUR KNITTING

If you can learn to read your knitting, it will help you immensely in all your projects, but especially when working in stitch patterns, whether they be textured, lace or colorwork.

What does it mean to read your knitting?

Reading your knitting means you can look at your knit fabric and for each individual stitch you can tell what it's doing, whether it's a knit or a purl stitch, a yarn over, an increase or a decrease, and so on. If you lose track of where you are in your stitch pattern—whether you've set your knitting down and then returned to it or simply drifted off in your mind—by reading the previous stitches or rows you can figure it out and be off and knitting again.

HOW TO DO IT

For the purposes of this book, let's look at three examples: reading knit and purl stitches in moss stitch, reading increases and decreases, and reading cables.

EXAMPLE: MOSS STITCH PATTERN

For this stitch pattern you are alternating knit and purl stitches, k1, p1, and so on. If you aren't sure if you last did a knit or a purl stitch, let's get up close and learn how to differentiate between the two stitches by sight.

(a) This is a knit stitch, which we easily recognize if we've knit in Stockinette stitch before. It's a smooth, flat "V".

(b) This stitch, the "V" with a bump of yarn wrapped in front of it, is a purl stitch. If you've worked in Stockinette stitch before, the wrong side (WS) or back of your sea of knit stitches are all purl sts.

EXAMPLE: DECREASES

When we decrease, we're taking stitches away so our knitting will get smaller. Different types of decreases appear differently. In this book we use SSK and k2tog.

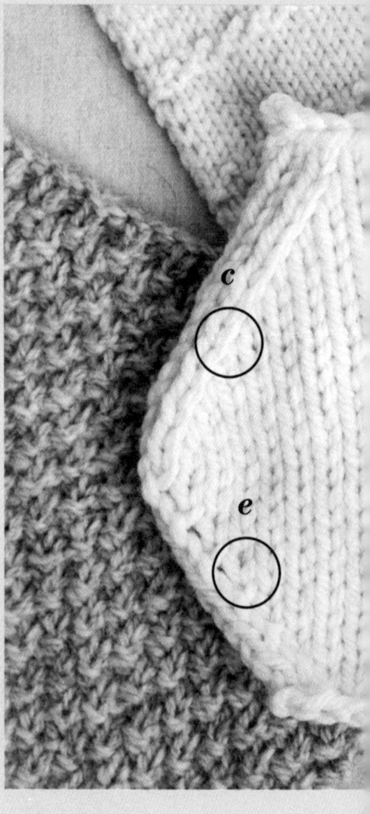

(c) K2tog: To work this decrease you simply knit two stitches together, as you would for one stitch. This decrease leans to the right.

(d) SSK: To work this decrease you slip a stitch as if to knit, again slip a stitch as if to knit, then knit these two sts together through the back. This decrease leans to the left.

EXAMPLE: INCREASES

When we increase, we're adding stitches so our knitting will grow. Different types of increases appear differently. In this book we use M1L and M1R.

(e) Make 1 left-slanting stitch (M1L): Between any two stitches there is a little bar of yarn. To work this increase, you lift the bar between stitches from front to back with the left needle. Knit through the back of it with the right needle. This increase leans to the left.

(f) Make 1 right-slanting stitch (M1R): Make one stitch by lifting the bar between stitches from back to front with the left needle. Knit through the front of the stitch with the right needle. This increase leans to the right.

EXAMPLE: HORSESHOE CABLE PATTERN

Cables can be tricky to read or measure because of their wave shape. At some points they are wider and then narrower. If we have an understanding of the entire pattern repeat, we can more easily study our cable. For this book, I chose the horseshoe cable because I felt it was the best for a beginner cabler. You only work one cable row, and you will work it every 8 rows or rounds.

(g) Here at the narrowest part of the cable is our cable row. For this cable we worked C4B, C4F.

(h1, h2) If the cable row is Row 1, from this point (h1) you can start counting the knit rows. There will be a total of 8 rows worked before you begin your next cable row (h2). If you aren't sure which row you're on, you can count from this point.

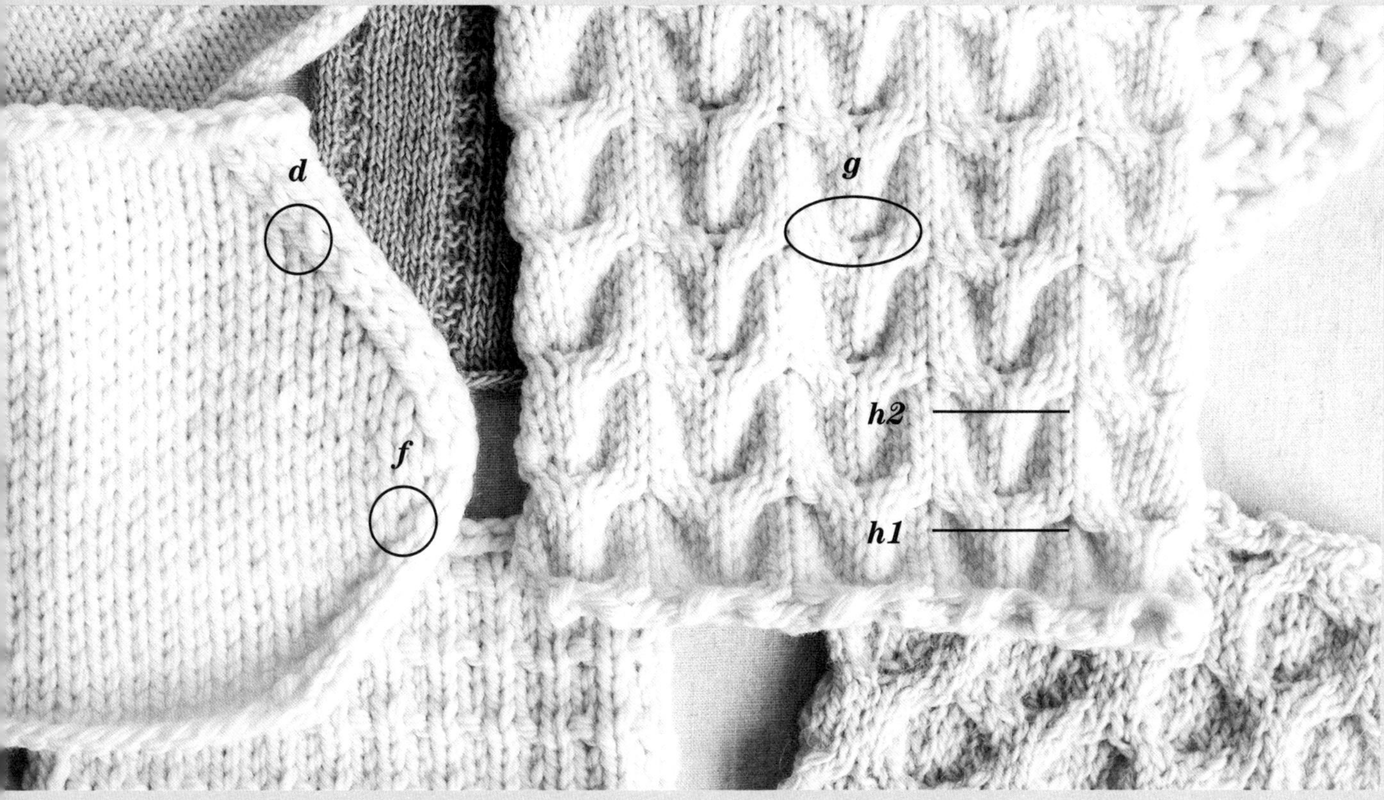

Go-to cardigan

Seamless

Statement collar

WORSTED WEIGHT YARN

WEST END CARDIGAN

I-CORD EDGING

ROW 1 (WS): Slip 1 stitch purlwise with yarn in front, knit 1, slip 1 stitch purlwise with yarn in front.

ROW 2 (RS): Knit 1, slip 1 stitch purlwise with yarn in front, k1.

HORSESHOE CABLE STITCH PATTERN

worked flat over 14 sts

ROWS 1, 3, 5 & 7 (WS): K1, p12, k1.

ROW 2 (RS): P1, C6B, C6F, p1.

ROWS 4, 6 & 8: P1, k12, p1.

MOSS STITCH PATTERN

worked flat over an odd number of sts

ROW 1 (RS): (K1, p1) repeat to last st, k1.

ROW 2 (WS): (P1, k1) repeat to last st, p1.

ROW 3: (P1, k1) repeat to last st, p1.

ROW 4: (K1, p1) repeat to last st, k1.

worked in the rnd over an even number of sts

RNDS 1 & 2: (K1, p1) repeat to end.

RNDS 3 & 4: (P1, k1) repeat to end.

body

BEGIN AT THE BOTTOM

Using smaller circular needle and a long-tail cast on, CO 149 (167, 185, 203, 221)[239, 257, 275, 293] sts.

ROW 1 (WS): Work i-cord edging over 3 sts, pm, k14, pm, p1, (k1, p1) to last 17 sts, pm, k14, pm, work i-cord edging over 3 sts.

ROW 2 (RS): Work i-cord edging over 3 sts, p1, k12, p1, (k1, p1) to 1 st before marker, k1, p1, k12, p1, work i-cord edging over 3 sts.

Cont as est for 2 rows more.

NEXT ROW (WS): Work i-cord edging over 3 sts, work Horseshoe Cable over 14 sts, work ribbing as est, work Horseshoe Cable over 14 sts, work i-cord edging over 3 sts.

Cont as est for 10 rows more, ending with a WS row.

Switch to larger circular needle.

NEXT ROW (RS): Work i-cord edging over 3 sts, work Horseshoe Cable over 14 sts, work in Moss Stitch patt to m, work Horseshoe Cable over 14 sts, work i-cord edging over 3 sts.

Cont as est until body meas 18 (18, 18.25, 18.75, 19.25)[19.75, 20.25, 20.75, 21.25]" / 45.5 (45.5, 46.5, 47.5, 49)[50, 51.5, 52.5, 54] cm, ending with a WS row, taking note of last row worked in Moss Stitch patt and Horseshoe Cable. Set aside.

sleeves

Using smaller circular needle and a long-tail cast on, CO 40 (42, 42, 44, 44)[46, 46, 48, 48] sts.

RIBBING SETUP ROW (RS): (K1, p1) repeat to end.

finished measurements

Chest circumference: 30 (34, 38.25, 42.5, 46.75) [51, 55.25, 59.25, 63.5]" / 76 (86.5, 97.5, 108, 118.5) [129.5, 140, 151, 161.5] cm

Shown in size 34" / 86.5 cm with no ease.

yarn

9 (10, 11, 12, 13)[15, 16, 17, 19] skeins Quince & Co. *Owl* (50% American wool, 50% alpaca; 120 yd / 110 m per 50 g skein) in Albertine

OR 975 (1125, 1250, 1400, 1550)[1700, 1850, 2025, 2200] yd / 875 (1025, 1150, 1275, 1425)[1575, 1700, 1875, 2025] m of worsted weight yarn

needles

US 7 / 4.5 mm:

- 32" / 80 cm circular needle

US 5 / 3.75 mm:

- 32" / 80 cm circular needle

Or size needed to obtain gauge.

notions

Stitch markers, cable needle, stitch holders or waste yarn, tapestry needle

gauge

19 sts and 32 rows = 4" / 10 cm in Moss Stitch pattern using larger needles

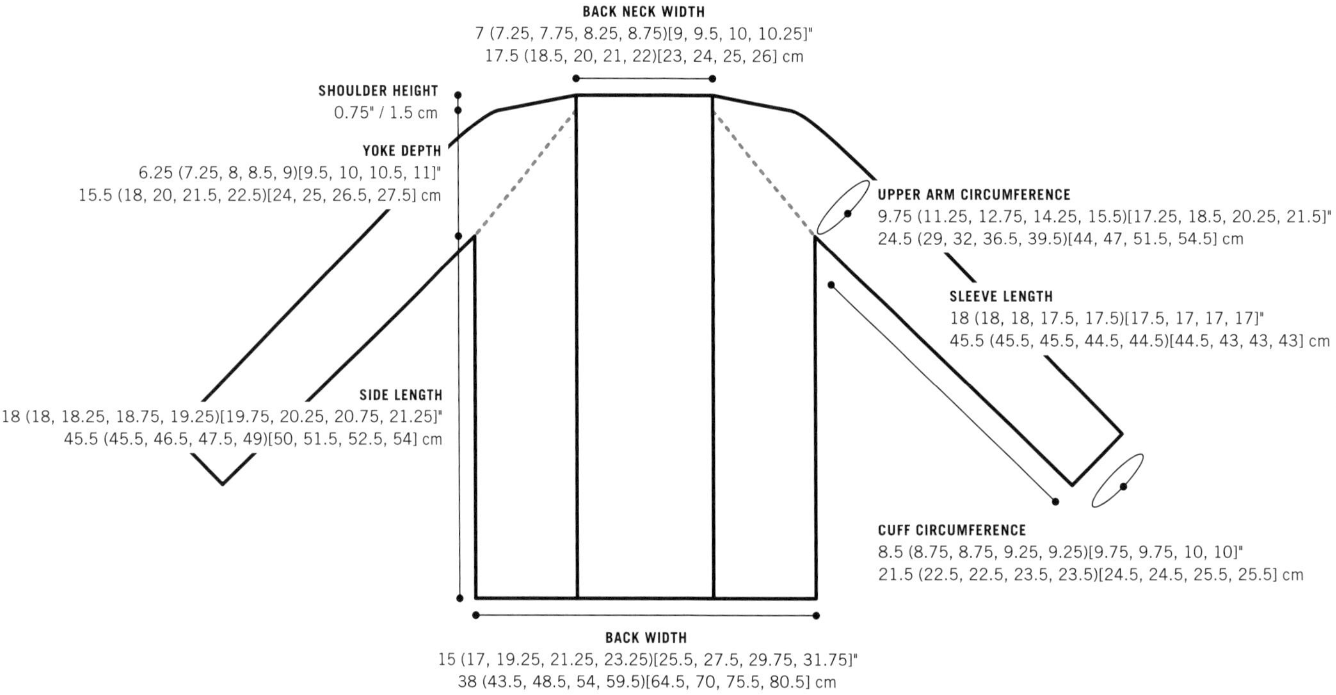

Cont in ribbing as est for 16 rows more.

Switch to larger circular needle.

NEXT ROW (WS): P1, work in Moss St to last st, p1.

INC ROW (RS): K1, M1L, work in Moss St to last st, M1R, k1. 2 sts inc.

Rep this inc row every 30 (20, 12, 8, 6)[4, 4, 4, 2] rows 2 (5, 6, 7, 8)[3, 14, 23, 6] times more, then every - (-, 14, 10, 8)[6, 6, -, 4] rows 0 (0, 2, 4, 6)[14, 6, 0, 20] times more. 46 (54, 60, 68, 74)[82, 88, 96, 102] sts.

Cont as est until sleeve meas 18 (18, 18, 17.5, 17.5)[17.5, 17, 17, 17]" / 45.5 (45.5, 45.5, 44.5, 44.5)[44.5, 43, 43, 43] cm or desired length, ending with same row of Moss Stitch patt as body. Place first and last 4 (5, 6, 7, 8)[9, 10, 11, 12] sts on a stitch holder. Transfer remaining 38 (44, 48, 54, 58)[64, 68, 74, 78] sleeve sts to a stitch holder.

Break yarn, leaving a tail 8–10" / 20–25 cm long. Set aside and repeat instructions for second sleeve.

Sew sleeve seams using Mattress Stitch.

yoke

JOIN BODY AND SLEEVES FOR YOKE

Return to body sts, ready to work a RS row.

NEXT ROW (RS): Work i-cord edging over 3 sts, work Horseshoe Cable as est over 14 sts, work 18 (21, 24, 27, 30)[33, 36, 39, 42] right front sts in Moss St as est, slip next 8 (10, 12, 14, 16)[18, 20, 22, 24] sts on a stitch holder for underarm, pm, work 38 (44, 48, 54, 58)[64, 68, 74, 78] sleeve sts in Moss St as est, pm, work 63 (71, 79, 87, 95)[103, 111, 119, 127] back sts in Moss St as est, slip next 8 (10, 12, 14, 16)[18, 20, 22, 24] sts on a stitch holder for underarm, pm, work 38 (44, 48, 54, 58)[64, 68, 74, 78] sleeve sts in Moss St as est, pm, work 18 (21, 24, 27, 30)[33, 36, 39, 42] left front sts in Moss St as est, work Horseshoe Cable as est over 14 sts, work i-cord edging over 3 sts. 209 (235, 257, 283, 305)[331, 353, 379, 401] sts: 35 (38, 41, 44, 47)[50, 53, 56, 59] front sts, 38 (44, 48, 54, 58)[64, 68, 74, 78] sleeve sts, 63 (71, 79, 87, 95)[103, 111, 119, 127] back sts.

NEXT ROW (WS): Work as est to 1 st before 3rd marker, * p1, sm, p1, work as est to 1 st before m; rep from * 3 times, work to end.

RAGLAN DEC ROW (RS): Work as est to 3 sts before 3rd marker, * k2tog, k1, sm, k1, ssk, work as est to 3 sts before m; rep from * 3 times, work to end. 8 sts dec.

Rep this dec row every RS row 5 (7, 9, 11, 13)[15, 17, 19, 21] times more. 161 (171, 177, 187, 193)[203, 209, 219, 225] sts: 29 (30, 31, 32, 33)[34, 35, 36, 37] front sts, 26 (28, 28, 30, 30)[32, 32, 34, 34] sleeve sts, 51 (55, 59, 63, 67)[71, 75, 79, 83] back sts.

Work 1 WS row.

FRONT AND SLEEVES ONLY DEC ROW (RS): Work to 3 sts before 3rd marker, k2tog, k1, sm, k1, ssk, work to 3 sts before m, k2tog, k1, sm, k1, work to 1 st before m, k1, sm, k1, ssk, work to 3 sts before m, k2tog, k1, sm, k1, ssk, work to end. 155 (165, 171, 181, 187)[197, 203, 213, 219] sts: 28 (29, 30, 31, 32)[33, 34, 35, 36] front sts, 24 (26, 26,

28, 28)[30, 30, 32, 32] sleeve sts, 51 (55, 59, 63, 67)[71, 75, 79, 83] back sts.

Work 1 WS row.

SIZES - (-, 38.25, 42.5, 46.75)[51, 55.25, 59.25, 63.5]" / - (-, 97.5, 108, 118.5)[129.5, 140, 151, 161.5] CM ONLY

FRONT AND BACK ONLY DEC ROW (RS): Work to 3 sts before 3rd marker, k2tog, k1, sm, k1, work to 1 st before m, k1, sm, k1, ssk, work to 3 sts before m, k2tog, k1, sm, k1, work to 1 st before m, k1, sm, k1, ssk, work to end. 4 sts dec.

Rep this dec row every RS row - (, 0, 0, 1)[1, 2, 2, 3] time(s) more. - (-, 167, 177, 179)[189, 191, 201, 203] sts: - (-, 29, 30, 30)[31, 31, 32, 32] front sts, - (-, 26, 28, 28)[30, 30, 32, 32] sleeve sts, - (-, 57, 61, 63)[67, 69, 73, 75] back sts.

Work 1 WS row even.

ALL SIZES

DEC ROW (RS): Work as est to 3 sts before 3rd marker, * k2tog, k1, sm, k1, ssk, work as est to 3 sts before m; rep from * 3 times, work to end. 8 sts dec.

Rep this dec row every RS row 0 (0, 0, 2, 3)[5, 6, 8, 9] times more, then every 4 rows 8 (9, 9, 8, 7)[6, 5, 4, 3] times more. 83 (85, 87, 89, 91) [93, 95, 97, 99] sts: 19 front sts, 6 sleeve sts, 33 (35, 37, 39, 41)[43, 45, 47, 49] back sts.

Work 1 WS row.

NEXT ROW (RS): Work 17 sts in patt then place on a stitch holder for right collar, then BO until 17 sts remain, work in patt to end.

finishing

COLLAR

Cont as est over 17 left front collar sts until collar meas 4.75 (5, 5.25, 5.25, 5.5)[5.75, 6, 6.25, 6.5]" / 12 (12.5, 13, 13.5, 14)[14.5, 15, 16, 16.5] cm from BO edge. Place sts on hold. Rep for right front collar. Join center back collar sts using 3-needle bind off or Kitchener Stitch.

Attach Collar side edge to BO edge at top of Sleeves and Back Neck using Mattress Stitch. Graft both sets of underarm stitches together using Kitchener Stitch.

Weave in all ends. Block to measurements.

CHOOSING YARN

Showcased in this book's designs are a selection of beautiful yarns produced by Quince & Company, based in Portland, Maine, and founded by Pam Allen in 2010.

Quince's line includes yarn made from 100% wool that is grown, processed, spun, dyed, twisted, and labeled in the USA. From fingering-weight *Finch* to bulky weight *Puffin*, each one is spun with the characteristics of fabric hand, stitch definition, and project gauge in mind. So many beautiful yarns in colors and natural shades I never tire of.

Quince has also created some great blends. *Owl* and *Owl Tweet* are fuzzy 2-ply woolen-spun wool/alpaca blends. *Piper* is a single-ply blend of laceweight Texas superfine merino and super kid mohair. Both *Owl* and *Piper* are featured in this book.

When designing, it was interesting to note the differences in textured stitches depending on yarn choice: round, smooth worsted-spun yarn versus woolen-spun, single-ply versus 2- or 3-ply. When considering substitute yarns, take a minute to consider what the original yarn is made of and how it's made. Then be sure to knit a nice big gauge swatch and check that you are happy with the resulting fabric compared with the original design.

Also, consider the difference color choice can make: pale, soft shades will allow all focus to be on the stitch pattern. Darker shades will give a more muted appearance to a textured fabric.

QUINCE & CO. YARNS FEATURED IN THIS BOOK

Piper
- 50/50 Texas superkid mohair/Texas superfine merino
- single-ply heavy laceweight
- grown, spun and dyed in the US

Finch
- 100% American wool
- 4-ply fingering weight
- grown, spun and dyed in the US

Tern
- 75/25 American wool/silk
- 3-ply fingering weight
- spun and dyed in the US

Sparrow
- 100% organic linen
- fingering weight
- made in Italy

Lark
- 100% American wool
- 4-ply worsted weight
- grown, spun and dyed in the US

Owl
- 50/50 American wool/alpaca
- worsted weight
- spun and dyed in the US

Osprey
- 100% American wool
- aran/heavy worsted weight
- grown, spun and dyed in the US

Puffin
- 100% American wool
- chunky/bulky weight
- grown, spun and dyed in the US

Modern classic

Cabled pullover

*Worked in
the round*

WORSTED WEIGHT YARN

WHARF STREET PULLOVER

HONEYCOMB STITCH PATTERN

worked in the rnd over 8 sts

RND 1: (C4B, C4F) repeat to end.

RNDS 2–6: Knit.

RND 7: (C4F, C4B) repeat to end.

RNDS 8–12: Knit.

worked flat over 8 sts

ROW 1 (RS): (C4B, C4F) repeat to end.

ROW 2 AND ALL WS ROWS: Purl.

ROWS 3 & 5: Knit.

ROW 7: (C4F, C4B) repeat to end.

ROWS 9 & 11: Knit.

ROW 12 (WS): Purl.

pattern note

In order to prevent cable splay, BO using the following method: K1, * (move st on right needle back to left needle, k2tog) twice, move st on right needle back to left needle, k3tog; rep from * until all sts have been bound off.

body

BEGIN AT THE BOTTOM

Using smaller circular needle and a long-tail cast on, CO 184 (208, 232, 256)[280, 304, 328, 352] sts. Join for working in the rnd, being careful to not twist sts. Pm to mark beg of the rnd.

RIBBING SETUP RND: (K1, p1) repeat to end.

Cont in ribbing as est for 3" / 7.5 cm.

Switch to larger circular needle.

Beg with Rnd 1 (5, 9, 1)[3, 5, 7, 9], work 108 (112, 116, 120)[122, 124, 126, 128] rnds of Honeycomb Stitch patt, ending with Rnd 8. Body meas approx 17.5 (18, 18.5, 19)[19.25, 19.5, 19.75, 20]" / 44.5 (45.5, 47, 48.5)[49, 49.5, 50, 51] cm.

Set aside.

sleeves

Using smaller dpns and a long-tail cast on, CO 50 (52, 54, 56)[58, 60, 62, 64] sts. Divide evenly over 3 dpns. Join for working in the rnd, being careful to not twist sts. Pm to mark beg of the rnd.

RIBBING SETUP RND: (K1, p1) repeat to end.

Cont in ribbing as est for 3" / 7.5 cm.

Switch to larger dpns.

NEXT RND: K1 (2, 3, 4)[1, 2, 3, 4], work in Honeycomb Stitch patt to last 1 (2, 3, 4)[1, 2, 3, 4] st(s), k1 (2, 3, 4)[1, 2, 3, 4].

INC RND: K1, M1L, k1, work in Honeycomb Stitch patt to last 2 sts, k1, M1R, k1.

finished measurements

Chest circumference: 32 (36.25, 40.25, 44.5)[48.75, 52.75, 57, 61.25]" / 81.5 (92, 102.5, 113)[123.5, 134.5, 145, 155.5] cm

Shown in size 36.25" / 92 cm with 2.25" / 5.5 cm of positive ease.

yarn

9 (10, 12, 13)[14, 16, 17, 19] skeins Quince & Co. *Owl* (50% American wool, 50% alpaca; 120 yd / 110 m per 50 g skein) in Abyssinian

OR 1050 (1175, 1325, 1475)[1650, 1825, 2025, 2200] yd / 950 (1075, 1225, 1350)[1525, 1675, 1850, 2025] m of worsted weight yarn

needles

US 8 / 5 mm:

- 32" / 80 cm circular needle
- set of double-pointed needles

US 6 / 4 mm:

- 32" / 80 cm circular needle
- set of double-pointed needles

Or size needed to obtain gauge.

notions

Stitch markers, cable needle, stitch holders or waste yarn, tapestry needle

gauge

23 sts and 30 rnds = 4" / 10 cm in Honeycomb Stitch pattern using larger needles; 1 cable pattern repeat (8 sts and 12 rnds) = 1.5" / 4 cm wide and 1.75" / 4.5 cm tall

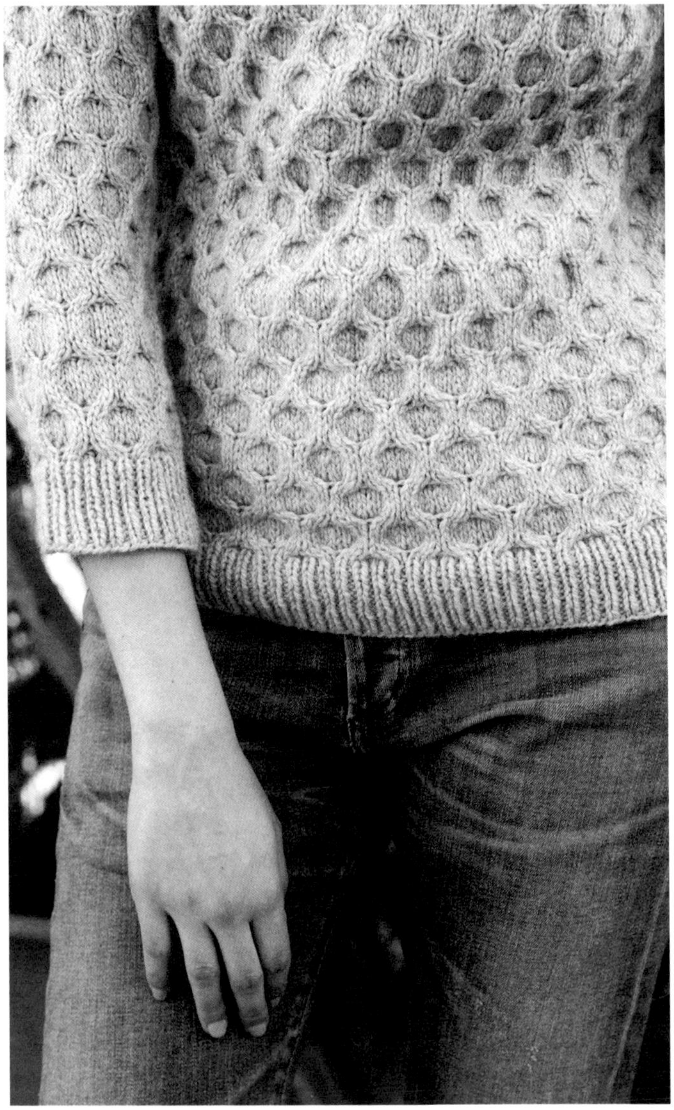

Cont as est, working additional sts in Honeycomb St as they become available, and rep inc rnd every 15 (10, 8, 6)[5, 5, 4, 3] rnds 1 (9, 1, 14)[16, 5, 18, 32] time(s) more, then every 14 (-, 7, 5)[4, 4, 3, 2] rnds 4 (0, 12, 3)[5, 20, 11, 1] time(s) more. 62 (72, 82, 92)[102, 112, 122, 132] sts.

Cont as est until 116 rnds of Honeycomb Stitch patt have been worked, ending with Rnd 8. Sleeve meas approx 18" / 45.5 cm. Place first and last 3 (4, 5, 6)[7, 8, 9, 10] sts on a stitch holder. Transfer remaining 56 (64, 72, 80)[88, 96, 104, 112] sleeve sts to a stitch holder.

Break yarn, leaving a tail 8–10" / 20–25 cm long. Set aside and repeat instructions for second sleeve.

yoke

JOIN BODY AND SLEEVES FOR YOKE

Return to body sts.

NEXT RND: Work 89 (100, 111, 122)[133, 144, 155, 166] front sts in stitch patt as est, slip next 6 (8, 10, 12)[14, 16, 18, 20] sts on a stitch holder for underarm, pm, work 56 (64, 72, 80)[88, 96, 104, 108] sleeve sts, pm, work 86 (96, 106, 116)[126, 136, 146, 154] back sts as est, slip next 6 (8, 10, 12)[14, 16, 18, 22] sts on a stitch holder for underarm, pm, work 56 (64, 72, 80)[88, 96, 104, 112] sleeve sts. 284 (320, 356, 392)[428, 464, 500, 536] sts: 86 (96, 106, 116)[126, 136, 146, 156] front and back sts, 56 (64, 72, 80)[88, 96, 104, 112] sleeve sts.
NEXT RND: (K1, work as est to 1 st before m, k1) 4 times, slipping markers as you come to them.

Work 4 (2, 0, 0)[0, 0, 0, 0] more rnds as est.

RAGLAN DEC RND: (K1, ssk, work as est to last 3 sts before m, k2tog, k1) 4 times, slipping markers as you come to them. 8 sts dec.

Rep this raglan dec rnd every rnd 0 (0, 2, 7)[9, 12, 14, 16] times more, then EOR 12 (16, 18, 17)[19, 20, 22, 24] times more. 180 (184, 188, 192)[196, 200, 204, 208] sts: 60 (62, 64, 66)[68, 70, 72, 74] front and back sts, 30 sleeve sts.

Work 1 rnd even.

NEXT RND: Work 19 sts as est, BO 22 (24, 26, 28)[30, 32, 34, 36] center neck sts, (work as est to 3 sts before m, k2tog, k1, sm, k1, ssk) 4 times, work to end. You will now work the yoke flat. 150 (152, 154, 156)[158, 160, 162, 164] sts: 18 front sts, 28 sleeve sts, 58 (60, 62, 64)[66, 68, 70, 72] back sts.
NEXT ROW (WS): Purl.

ROW 1—RAGLAN AND NECK DEC ROW (RS): (K1, ssk, work as est to 3 sts before m, k2tog, k1) 5 times, slipping markers as you come to them. 10 sts dec.
ROW 2 (WS): Purl.
ROW 3—BODY ONLY DEC ROW: Work to 3 sts before m, k2tog, k1, sm, work to m, sm, k1, ssk, work to 3 sts before m, k2tog, k1, sm, work to m, sm, k1, ssk, work to end. 4 sts dec.

ROW 4: Purl.

Rep these 4 rows 4 times more. 80 (82, 84, 86)[88, 90, 92, 94] sts: 3 front sts, 18 sleeve sts, 38 (40, 42, 44)[46, 48, 50, 52] back sts.

BO remaining sts.

finishing

NECKBAND

Using smaller circular needle, pick up and knit 63 (64, 66, 67)[69, 70, 72, 73] sts along BO edge, 16 sts along left side neck, 17 (18, 20, 21)[23, 24, 26, 27] sts along center front neck, and 16 sts along right side neck. Pm to mark beg of the rnd. 112 (114, 118, 120)[124, 126, 130, 132] sts.

RIBBING SETUP RND: (K1, p1) repeat to end.

Cont in ribbing as est for 10 rnds more.

BO loosely in ribbing.

Graft both sets of underarm stitches together using Kitchener Stitch.

Weave in all ends. Block to measurements.

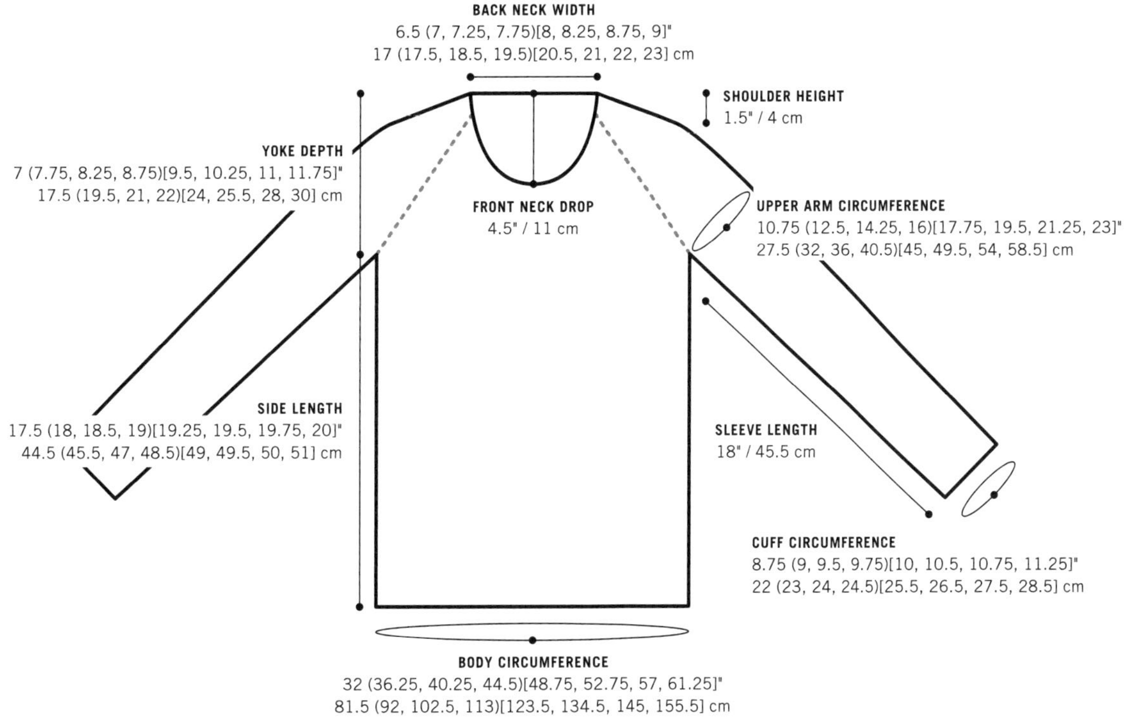

BACK NECK WIDTH
6.5 (7, 7.25, 7.75)[8, 8.25, 8.75, 9]"
17 (17.5, 18.5, 19.5)[20.5, 21, 22, 23] cm
SHOULDER HEIGHT
1.5" / 4 cm
YOKE DEPTH
7 (7.75, 8.25, 8.75)[9.5, 10.25, 11, 11.75]"
17.5 (19.5, 21, 22)[24, 25.5, 28, 30] cm
FRONT NECK DROP
4.5" / 11 cm
UPPER ARM CIRCUMFERENCE
10.75 (12.5, 14.25, 16)[17.75, 19.5, 21.25, 23]"
27.5 (32, 36, 40.5)[45, 49.5, 54, 58.5] cm
SIDE LENGTH
17.5 (18, 18.5, 19)[19.25, 19.5, 19.75, 20]"
44.5 (45.5, 47, 48.5)[49, 49.5, 50, 51] cm
SLEEVE LENGTH
18" / 45.5 cm
CUFF CIRCUMFERENCE
8.75 (9, 9.5, 9.75)[10, 10.5, 10.75, 11.25]"
22 (23, 24, 24.5)[25.5, 26.5, 27.5, 28.5] cm
BODY CIRCUMFERENCE
32 (36.25, 40.25, 44.5)[48.75, 52.75, 57, 61.25]"
81.5 (92, 102.5, 113)[123.5, 134.5, 145, 155.5] cm

INCREASING AND DECREASING IN STITCH PATTERN

When we use increases our knit fabric will grow. When we use decreases our knit fabric will shrink. In either case, our textured stitch pattern is affected. In this section we'll talk about how to maintain a stitch pattern in these scenarios.

RAGLAN YOKE

When working increases or decreases in a raglan yoke, we maintain two stitches of Stockinette stitch at the raglan line. This makes incorporating stitch pattern as the piece grows or shrinks a little more straightforward.

Increase example: Raglan increases for a top down cardigan.

> (right front) Work in stitch pattern to 1 st from m, M1L, k1, sm, (sleeve) k1, M1L work in stitch pattern to one st from m, M1R, k1, sm, (back) k1, M1L, work in stitch pattern to 1 st from m, M1R, k1, sm, (sleeve) k1, M1L, work in stitch pattern to 1 st from m, M1R, k1, sm, (left front) k1, M1L, work in stitch pattern to end.

This increase row is repeated as you work the yoke. Note that it says to work in stitch pattern between increases and raglan lines. As the yoke grows, you incorporate the stitch pattern as shown.

SLEEVE

When working sleeves in the round, we do not include knit stitches between the increases or decreases as we did for the raglan, as here it would look strange to have a "stripe" of knit stitches in the middle of the stitch pattern. However, if we are knitting the sleeves flat we will include one knit stitch on each end for seaming. See page 90 for more on that.

Decrease example: Sleeves worked from the top down.

> Ssk, work to last 2 sts, k2tog.

This decrease row is worked every inch or so down the underside of the sleeve.

As the sleeve gets smaller in circumference, incorporate the stitch pattern as shown.

DON'T LEAVE ME HANGING

In most cases it's best not to incorporate a partial stitch repeat. In the case of cables, once you have enough stitches to work half of a cable you can do so. For example, the full cable repeat for the *Pierside Cardigan* (page 76) is C8B, C8F. If you are increasing, once you have 8 stitches you may work C8B or C8F. Once you have increased to 16 stitches you can work the entire cable. Until then work extra stitches in Stockinette stitch.

HOW TO KEEP TRACK

A visual aid can be helpful. Use graph paper and chart out the stitch pattern with the raglan increases or decreases.

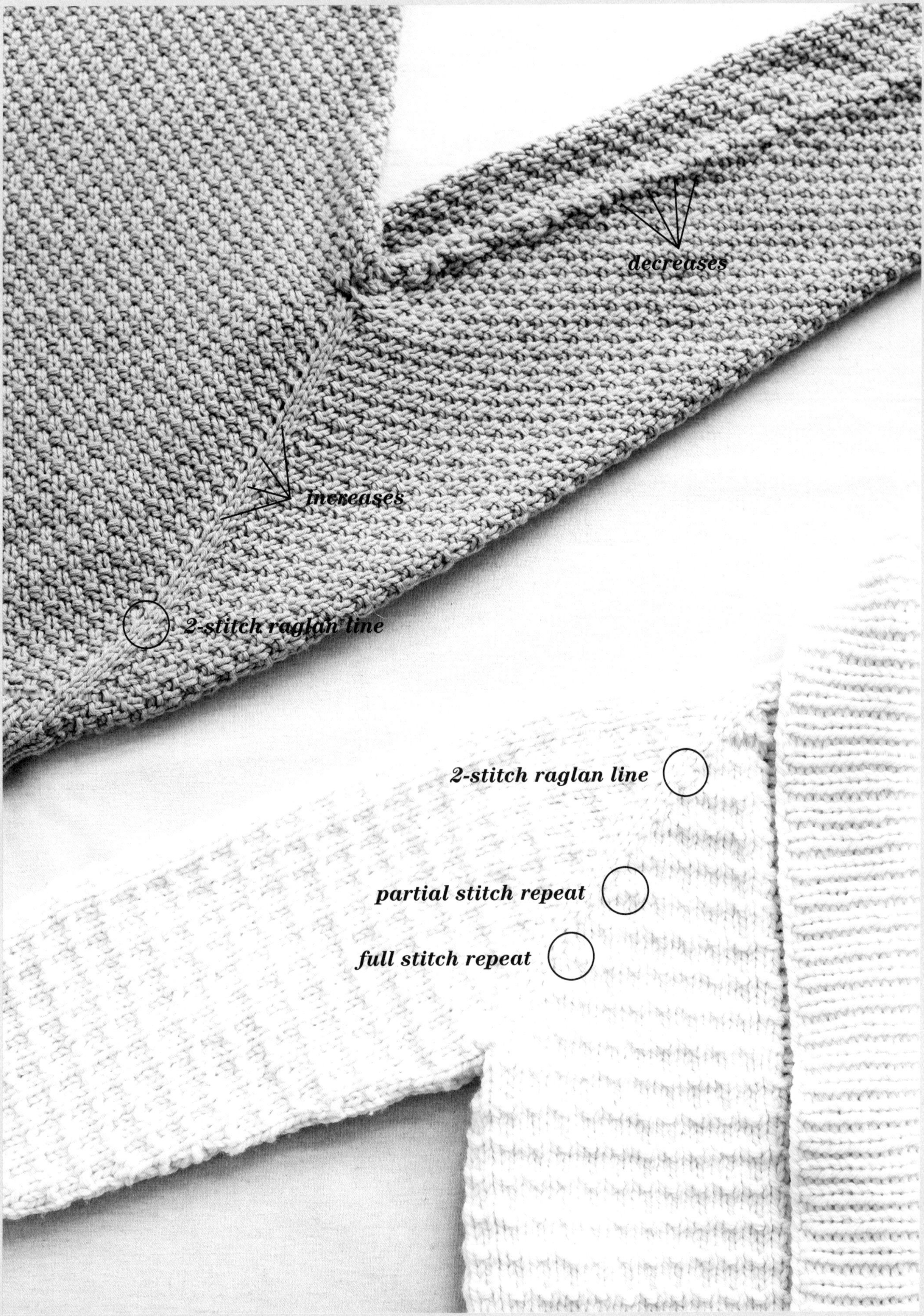
decreases
increases
2-stitch raglan line
2-stitch raglan line
partial stitch repeat
full stitch repeat

Seasonal set

Simple pattern repeat

2-skein project

WORSTED WEIGHT YARN

TEXTURED HAT & MITTS SET

MAINE

TEXTURED STITCH PATTERN

worked in the rnd over 8 sts

RNDS 1 & 2: Knit.

RNDS 3 & 4: (P2, k6) repeat to end.

RNDS 5 & 6: Knit.

RNDS 7 & 8: K4, (p2, k6) repeat to last 4 sts, p2, k2.

mitts

BEGIN AT CUFF

With smaller dpns and using a tubular cast on, CO 36 sts. Divide sts evenly over 3 dpns. Join for working in the rnd, being careful not to twist sts. Pm to mark beg of the rnd.

RIBBING SETUP RND: (K1, p1) repeat to end.

Cont in ribbing as est for 9 rnds more.

Switch to larger dpns.

NEXT RND: K1, work in Textured Stitch patt over 16 sts, pm, k2, pm, work in Textured Stitch patt to last st, k1.

BEGIN THUMB GUSSET

INC RND: K1, work in Textured Stitch patt to m, sm, M1L, knit to m, M1R, sm, work in Textured Stitch patt to last st, k1. 2 sts inc.

Rep this inc rnd every 3 rnds 4 times more. 46 sts.

Work 2 rnds even.

DIVIDE THUMB FROM MITT

NEXT RND: Work as est to m, place 12 thumb sts on a stitch holder, using a backward loop cast on, CO 2 sts over gap, sm, work to end. 36 sts.

Work 4 rnds.

Switch to smaller dpns.

RIBBING SETUP RND: (K1, p1) repeat to end.

Cont in ribbing as est for 6 rnds more.

BO loosely in ribbing.

FINISH THUMB

Divide 12 held thumb sts evenly over 3 smaller dpns. Pick up and knit 2 sts along edge of gap. Pm to mark beg of the rnd.
14 sts.

RIBBING SETUP RND: (K1, p1) repeat to end.

Cont in ribbing as est for 6 rnds more.

BO loosely in ribbing.

mitts finishing

Weave in all ends. Block to measurements.

finished measurements

Mitts: 7.25" [18.5 cm] hand circumference and 5" [13 cm] long

Hat: 19.25" / 49 cm circumference

yarn

2 skeins Quince & Co. *Owl* (50% American wool, 50% alpaca; 120 yd / 110m per 50 g skein) in Elf

OR 125 yd / 100 m of worsted weight yarn for hat, 100 yd / 100 m for mitts

needles

US 7 / 4.5 mm:

- 16" / 40 cm circular needle
- set of double-pointed needles

US 5 / 3.75 mm:

- 16" / 40 cm circular needle
- set of double-pointed needles

Or size needed to obtain gauge.

notions

Stitch markers, stitch holders or waste yarn, tapestry needle

gauge

20 sts and 28 rnds = 4" / 10 cm in St st using larger needles

hat

Using smaller circular needle and a long-tail cast on, CO 96 sts. Join for working in the rnd, being careful to not twist sts. Pm to mark beg of the rnd.

RIBBING SETUP RND: (K1, p1) repeat to end.

Cont in ribbing as est for 2" / 5 cm.

Switch to larger circular needle.

Begin working in Textured Stitch patt. Cont until hat meas 6.5" / 16.5 cm, ending with Rnd 6 of Textured Stitch patt.

DEC RND: (K4, p2, k2tog) repeat to end. 84 sts.
NEXT RND: (K4, p2, k1) repeat to end.
DEC RND: (K5, k2tog) repeat to end. 72 sts.
NEXT RND: Knit.
DEC RND: (P2, k2, k2tog) repeat to end. 60 sts.
NEXT RND: (P2, k3) repeat to end.
DEC RND: (K3, k2tog) repeat to end. 48 sts.
NEXT RND: Knit.
DEC RND: (K2, k2tog) repeat to end. 36 sts.
NEXT RND: Knit.
DEC RND: (K1, k2tog) repeat to end. 24 sts.
NEXT RND: Knit.
DEC RND: (K2tog) repeat to end. 12 sts.
NEXT RND: Knit.
DEC RND: (K2tog) repeat to end. 6 sts.

hat finishing

Break yarn leaving a tail. Weave through remaining 6 sts and pull tight. Weave end into WS of hat.

Weave in remaining ends.

Block to measurements.

BIG TEXTURE

FABRIC PROPERTIES: This section features BIG, exaggerated texture. When you enlarge a stitch pattern to 3 or 4 stitches per inch it really takes over. All-over cables can create a dense fabric, so even a worsted gauge garment can get bumped from everyday wear to outerwear. The fabric will be eye catching, a statement piece perhaps.

GARMENTS WELL SUITED FOR: All-over texture at a large gauge can be great for a jacket, oversized cardigan, or pullover. Maybe it's something you'll wear mostly at home, or outside on an extra cool day. Large scale texture is fantastic for cowls. In certain seasons you might get everyday wear out of this accessory, like the cowls on page 98.

YARN: You may go for a super-soft single-ply big wool, like Quince & Co *Puffin*. If you're not wearing it everyday, pilling will not be as much of a concern. Or a plied yarn with a loose twist, like Quince & Co. *Osprey*, which creates an airy, squishy fabric. No matter what you use, those textured stitches are going to pop!

Simple cable repeat

Structured with set-in sleeve and seams

Casual oversize collar

WORSTED WEIGHT YARN

CARDIGAN

CABLE STITCH PATTERN
worked flat over 16 sts
ROW 1 (RS): (C8B, C8F) repeat to end.
ROWS 2–8: Knit on the RS, purl on the WS.

notes

In order to prevent cable splay, BO using the following method: K1, * (move st on right needle back to left needle, k2tog) twice, move st on right needle back to left needle, k3tog; rep from * until all sts have been bound off.

body

BEGIN AT THE BOTTOM
Using smaller circular needle and a long-tail cast on, CO 163 (187, 211, 235, 259)[283, 307, 331, 355] sts.

RIBBING SETUP ROW (RS): (K1, p1) repeat to last st, k1.

Cont in ribbing as est for 12 rows more, ending with a RS row.

Switch to larger needles.

DEC ROW (WS): Purl to last 4 sts, p2tog, p2. 162 (186, 210, 234, 258) [282, 306, 330, 354] sts.
NEXT ROW (RS): K1 (5, 1, 5, 1)[5, 1, 5, 1], work Row 1 of Cable Stitch patt until 1 (5, 1, 5, 1)[5, 1, 5, 1] st(s) rem, k1 (5, 1, 5, 1)[5, 1, 5, 1].

Cont in Cable Stitch patt as est until body meas 16.5 (17, 17.5, 18, 18.5)[19, 19.5, 20, 20.5]" / 42 (43, 44.5, 45.5, 47)[48.5, 49.5, 51, 52] cm or desired length, ending with a WS row.

SHAPE ARMHOLE
NEXT ROW (RS): Work 23 (28, 32, 37, 41)[46, 50, 55, 59] right front sts, BO 10 (12, 14, 16, 18)[20, 22, 24, 26] armhole sts, work 96 (106, 118, 128, 140)[150, 162, 172, 184] back sts, BO 10 (12, 14, 16, 18) [20, 22, 24, 26] armhole sts, work 23 (28, 32, 37, 41)[46, 50, 55, 59] left front sts to end. Place back and right front sts on stitch holders, noting last row worked in Cable Stitch patt.

left front

Work 1 WS row even.

DEC ROW (RS): K2, k2tog, work in Cable Stitch patt as est to end. 1 st dec.

Rep this dec row every RS row 0 (3, 6, 10, 13)[17, 20, 24, 26] times more. 22 (24, 25, 26, 27)[28, 29, 30, 32] sts.

Cont as est until armhole meas 6.5 (7, 7.5, 8, 8.5)[9, 9.5, 10, 10.5]" / 16.5 (18, 19, 20.5, 21.5)[23, 24, 25.5, 26.5] cm, ending with a WS row.

SHAPE SHOULDER
NEXT ROW (RS): BO 12 (12, 13, 13, 14)[14, 15, 15, 16] sts, work to end.

Work 1 WS row.

finished measurements

Chest circumference: 32.5 (36.25, 40.5, 44.25, 48.5) [52.25, 56.5, 60.25, 64.5]" / 83 (92, 103, 112.5, 123.5) [133, 144, 153, 164] cm
Shown in 36.25" / 92 cm with 2.25" / 5.5 cm of positive ease.

yarn

13 (14, 16, 17, 19)[20, 22, 24, 25] skeins Quince & Co. *Lark* (100% American wool; 134 yd / 123 m per 50 g skein) in Iceland

OR 1675 (1850, 2025, 2275, 2450)[2650, 2925, 3125, 3325] yd / 1550 (1700, 1850, 2075, 2250) [2425, 2675, 2875, 3050] m of worsted weight yarn

needles

US 8 / 5 mm:
- 32" / 80 cm circular needle
- set of double-pointed needles

US 6 / 4 mm:
- 16" / 40 cm circular needle
- 32" / 80 cm circular needle
- set of double-pointed needles

Or size needed to obtain gauge.

notions

Cable needle, stitch holders or waste yarn, tapestry needle

gauge

26 sts and 32 rows = 4" / 10 cm in Cable Stitch pattern using larger needles; 1 cable repeat (16 sts and 8 rows) = 2.25" / 6 cm wide and 1" / 2.5 cm tall

BO remaining 11 (12, 12, 13, 13)[14, 14, 15, 16] sts.

right front

Place 23 (28, 32, 37, 41)[46, 50, 55, 59] held right front sts on needles, ready to work a WS row.

Work 1 WS row even.

DEC ROW (RS): Work in Cable Stitch patt as est to last 4 sts, ssk, k2. 1 st dec.

Rep this dec row every RS row 0 (3, 6, 10, 13)[17, 20, 24, 26] times. 22 (24, 25, 26, 27)[28, 29, 30, 32] sts.

Cont as est until armhole meas 6.5 (7, 7.5, 8, 8.5)[9, 9.5, 10, 10.5]" / 16.5 (18, 19, 20.5, 21.5)[23, 24, 25.5, 26.5] cm, ending with a RS row.

SHAPE SHOULDER

NEXT ROW (WS): BO 12 (12, 13, 13, 14)[14, 15, 15, 16] sts, work to end.

Work 1 WS row.

BO remaining 11 (12, 12, 13, 13)[14, 14, 15, 16] sts.

back

Place 96 (106, 118, 128, 140)[150, 162, 172, 184] held back sts on needles, ready to work a WS row.

Work 1 WS row even.

DEC ROW (RS): K2, k2tog, work in Cable Stitch patt as est to last 4 sts, ssk, k2. 2 sts dec.

Rep this dec row every RS row 0 (3, 6, 10, 13)[17, 20, 24, 26] times more. 94 (98, 104, 106, 112)[114, 120, 122, 130] sts.

Cont as est until armhole meas 6.5 (7, 7.5, 8, 8.5)[9, 9.5, 10, 10.5]" / 16.5 (18, 19, 20.5, 21.5)[23, 24, 25.5, 26.5] cm, ending with a WS row.

SHAPE SHOULDERS

BO 12 (12, 13, 13, 14)[14, 15, 15, 16] sts at beg of next 2 rows, then BO 11 (12, 12, 13, 13)[14, 14, 15, 16] sts at beg of next 2 rows. BO 50 (50, 54, 54, 58)[58, 62, 62, 66] rem back neck sts.

sleeves

Using smaller needle and a long-tail cast on, CO 56 (58, 60, 62, 64)[66, 68, 70, 72] sts.

RIBBING SETUP ROW (RS): (K1, p1) repeat to end.

Cont in ribbing as est for 4" / 10 cm, ending with a RS row.

Switch to larger needles.

Work 1 WS row even.

INC ROW (RS): K1, M1L, work in Cable Stitch patt to last st, M1R, k1. 2 sts inc.

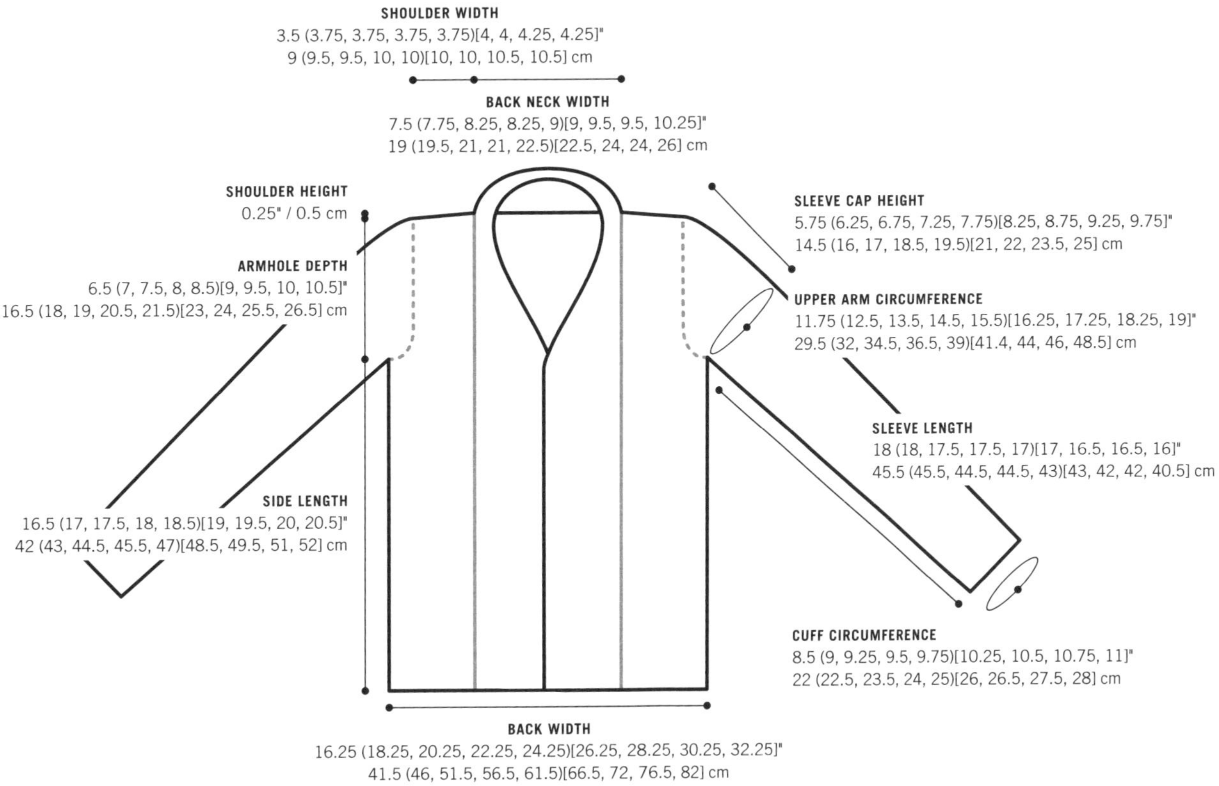
SHOULDER WIDTH
3.5 (3.75, 3.75, 3.75, 3.75)[4, 4, 4.25, 4.25]"
9 (9.5, 9.5, 10, 10)[10, 10, 10.5, 10.5] cm
BACK NECK WIDTH
7.5 (7.75, 8.25, 8.25, 9)[9, 9.5, 9.5, 10.25]"
19 (19.5, 21, 21, 22.5)[22.5, 24, 24, 26] cm
SHOULDER HEIGHT
0.25" / 0.5 cm
ARMHOLE DEPTH
6.5 (7, 7.5, 8, 8.5)[9, 9.5, 10, 10.5]"
16.5 (18, 19, 20.5, 21.5)[23, 24, 25.5, 26.5] cm
SIDE LENGTH
16.5 (17, 17.5, 18, 18.5)[19, 19.5, 20, 20.5]"
42 (43, 44.5, 45.5, 47)[48.5, 49.5, 51, 52] cm
SLEEVE CAP HEIGHT
5.75 (6.25, 6.75, 7.25, 7.75)[8.25, 8.75, 9.25, 9.75]"
14.5 (16, 17, 18.5, 19.5)[21, 22, 23.5, 25] cm
UPPER ARM CIRCUMFERENCE
11.75 (12.5, 13.5, 14.5, 15.5)[16.25, 17.25, 18.25, 19]"
29.5 (32, 34.5, 36.5, 39)[41.4, 44, 46, 48.5] cm
SLEEVE LENGTH
18 (18, 17.5, 17.5, 17)[17, 16.5, 16.5, 16]"
45.5 (45.5, 44.5, 44.5, 43)[43, 42, 42, 40.5] cm
CUFF CIRCUMFERENCE
8.5 (9, 9.25, 9.5, 9.75)[10.25, 10.5, 10.75, 11]"
22 (22.5, 23.5, 24, 25)[26, 26.5, 27.5, 28] cm
BACK WIDTH
16.25 (18.25, 20.25, 22.25, 24.25)[26.25, 28.25, 30.25, 32.25]"
41.5 (46, 51.5, 56.5, 61.5)[66.5, 72, 76.5, 82] cm

Cont in patt as est, working additional sts in Cable Stitch patt as they become available, and rep inc row every 10 (8, 6, 6, 4)[4, 4, 2, 2] rows 5 (6, 5, 13, 6)[12, 20, 3, 9] times more, then every 12 (10, 8, 8, 6)[6, 6, 4, 4] rows 4 (5, 8, 2, 11)[7, 1, 20, 16] times more. 76 (82, 88, 94, 100)[106, 112, 118, 124] sts.

Cont as est until sleeve meas 18 (18, 17.5, 17.5, 17)[17, 16.5, 16.5, 16]" / 45.5 (45.5, 44.5, 44.5, 43)[43, 42, 42, 40.5] cm or desired length, ending with a WS row.

SHAPE CAP

BO 5 (6, 7, 8, 9)[10, 11, 12, 13] sts at beg of next 2 rows.

DEC ROW (RS): K1, k2tog, work as est to last 3 sts, ssk, k1. 2 sts dec.

Rep this dec row every RS row 19 (21, 23, 25, 27)[29, 31, 33, 35] times more. 26 sts.

Work 1 WS row even.

BO 2 sts at beg of next 2 rows, then 3 sts at beg of next 2 rows.

BO remaining 16 sts.

finishing

Join shoulder seams.

COLLAR

Using smaller needles and beg at the bottom right edge, pick up and knit 2 sts for every 3 rows up the right front of the cardigan, pick up and knit evenly across back neck, then pick up and knit 2 sts for every 3 rows down the left front. Adjust, if needed, so there is an odd number of sts.

RIBBING SETUP ROW (WS): (K1, p1) repeat to last st, k1.

Continue in ribbing as est for 4 (4, 4, 4.5, 4.5)[4.5, 5, 5, 5]" / 10 (10, 10, 11.5, 11.5)[11.5, 12.5, 12.5, 12.5] cm.

Switch to larger needles.

Cont in ribbing until collar meas 8 (8, 8, 9, 9)[9, 10, 10, 10]" / 20.5 (20.5, 20.5, 23, 23)[23, 25.5, 25.5, 25.5] cm.

BO loosely in ribbing.

Sew cap into armhole. Sew sleeve seams using Mattress Stitch.

Weave in all ends. Block to measurements.

DIVIDING SLEEVES FROM BODY

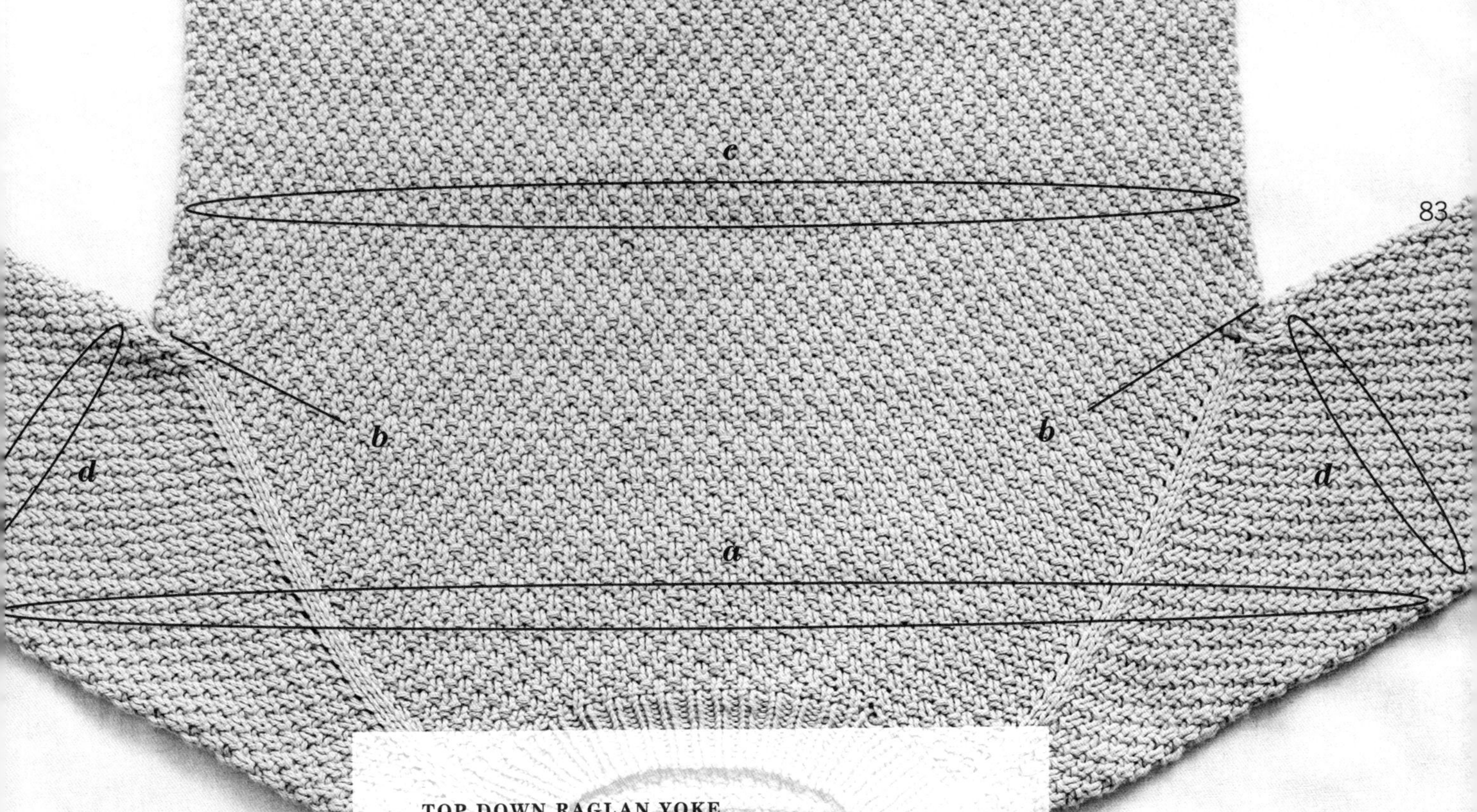

TOP DOWN RAGLAN YOKE

(a) Once yoke is complete, you separate the sleeve sts and place them on a stitch holder. *(b)* Underarm stitches are cast on. *(c)* The body is worked until complete. *(d)* Then place sleeve stitches on needles and work.

BOTTOM UP RAGLAN YOKE

(e) Body stitches are worked until underarm edge. Place body stitches on a stitch holder. *(f)* Knit two sleeves until underarm edge and place on stitch holders. *(g)* Then join sleeve and body stitches together and begin knitting the yoke.

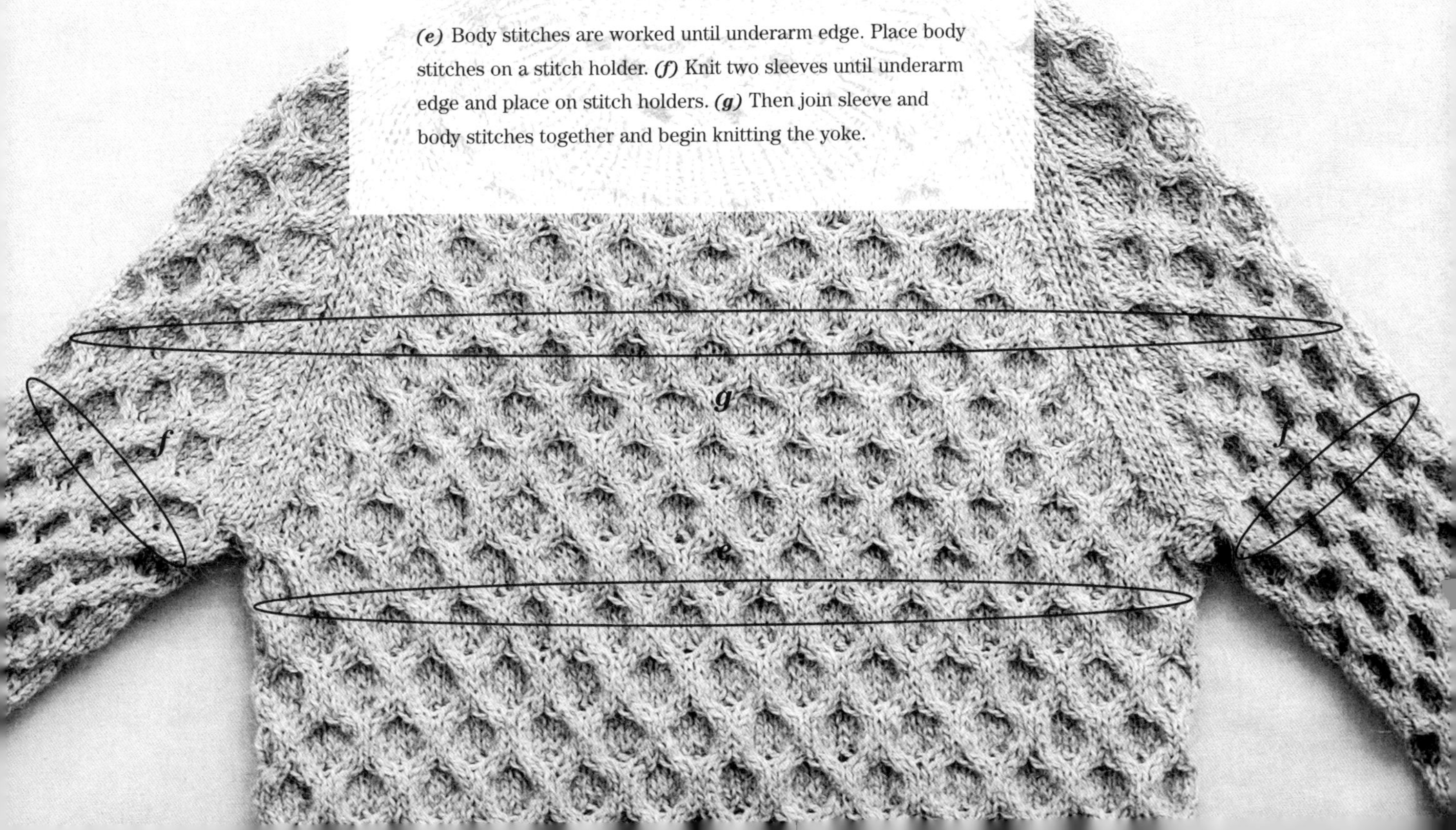

Cropped raglan cardi

Textured stripes

Open front

ARAN WEIGHT YARN

ART WALK
CARDI

ART

STITCH PATTERN

worked flat over an odd number of sts

ROW 1 (RS): Knit.

ROW 2 (WS): Purl.

ROW 3: (K1, p1) repeat to last st, k1.

ROW 4: Purl.

worked in the rnd over an odd number of sts

RNDS 1 & 2: Knit.

RND 3: (K1, p1) repeat to last st, k1.

RND 4: Knit.

yoke

BEGIN AT THE TOP

Using larger circular needle and a long-tail cast on, CO 43 (45, 47, 49, 51)[53, 55, 57, 59] sts.

SETUP ROW (WS): P3, pm, p5, pm, p27 (29, 31, 33, 35)[37, 39, 41, 43], pm, p5, pm, p3.

ESTABLISH RAGLAN INCREASES AND STITCH PATTERN

INC ROW (RS): * Work in Stitch patt to 1 st before m, M1R, k1, sm, k1, M1L; rep from * 3 times more, work in Stitch patt to end. 8 sts inc.

Rep this inc row every RS row 17 (19, 21, 23, 25)[27, 29, 31, 33] times more. 187 (205, 223, 241, 259)[277, 295, 313, 331] sts: 21 (23, 25, 27, 29)[31, 33, 35, 37] fronts, 41 (45, 49, 53, 57)[61, 65, 69, 73] sleeves, 63 (69, 75, 81, 87)[93, 99, 105, 111] back.

Work 1 WS row. Yoke meas approx 6.25 (6.75, 7.5, 8.25, 8.75)[9.5, 10.25, 10.75, 11.5]" / 15.5 (17.5, 19, 20.5, 22.5)[24, 26, 27.5, 29] cm.

DIVIDE SLEEVES FROM BODY

NEXT ROW (RS): * Work as est to m, removing markers, place 41 (45, 49, 53, 57)[61, 65, 69, 73] sleeve sts on a stitch holder, using a backward loop cast on, CO 3 (5, 7, 9, 11)[13, 15, 17, 19] underarm sts; rep from * once more, work as est to end. 111 (125, 139, 153, 167)[181, 195, 209, 223] sts.

Cont as est until body meas 14.75 (15, 15.25, 15.75, 16)[16.25, 16.75, 17, 17.25]" / 37.5 (38, 38.5, 40, 40.5)[41.5, 42.5, 43, 44] cm from underarm, or 3" / 7.5 cm shorter than desired length, ending with a WS row.

Switch to smaller circular needle.

RIBBING SETUP ROW (RS): (K1, p1) repeat to last st , k1.

Cont in ribbing as est for 17 rows more.

BO loosely in ribbing.

sleeves

Divide 41 (45, 49, 53, 57)[61, 65, 69, 73] held sleeve sts evenly over 3 larger dpns. Using a 4th dpn, pick up and knit 2 (3, 4, 5, 6)[7, 8, 9, 10] sts along underarm edge, pm, pick up and knit 1 (2, 3, 4, 5)[6, 7, 8, 9]

finished measurements

Chest circumference: 33 (37, 41, 45, 49)[53, 57, 61, 65]" / 84 (94, 104, 114.5, 124.5)[134.5, 145, 155, 165] cm

Shown in size 37" / 94 cm with 3" / 7.5 cm of positive ease.

yarn

6 (7, 8, 9, 10)[10, 12, 12, 13] skeins Quince & Co. *Osprey* (100% American wool; 170 yd / 155 m per 100 g skein) in Egret

OR 1000 (1100, 1250, 1400, 1575)[1700, 1875, 2025, 2200] yd / 900 (1025, 1150, 1275, 1425)[1550, 1725, 1850, 2000] m of aran weight yarn

needles

US 10 / 6 mm:

- 32" / 80 cm circular needle
- set of double-pointed needles

US 9 / 5.5 mm:

- 32" / 80 cm circular needle
- set of double-pointed needles

Or size needed to obtain gauge.

notions

Stitch markers, stitch holders or waste yarn, tapestry needle

gauge

16 sts and 24 rows = 4" / 10 cm in Stitch pattern using larger needles

st(s) along underarm edge, join for working in the rnd. 44 (50, 56, 62, 68)[74, 80, 86, 92] sts.

Work in Stitch patt as est for 14 (10, 8, 6, 5)[4, 4, 3, 3] rnds.

DEC RND: K1, ssk, work to last 3 sts, k2tog, k1. 2 sts dec.

Rep this dec rnd every 15 (11, 9, 7, 6)[5, 5, 4, 4] rnds 4 (6, 2, 10, 10) [12, 3, 15, 15] times more, then every - (-, 8, 6, 5)[4, 4, 3, 3] rnds 0 (0, 7, 1, 3)[4, 15, 5, 18] time(s) more. 34 (36, 36, 38, 40)[40, 42, 44, 44] sts.

Cont as est until sleeve meas 15 (15, 14.75, 14.75, 14.5)[14.5, 14.25, 14.25, 14]" / 38 (38, 37.5, 37.5, 37)[37, 36, 36, 35.5] cm from underarm, or 3" / 7.5 cm shorter than desired length.

Switch to smaller dpns.

RIBBING SETUP RND: (K1, p1) repeat to end.

Cont in ribbing as est for 17 rnds more.

BO loosely in ribbing.

finishing

COLLAR

Using smaller circular needle and beginning at bottom edge, pick up and knit 2 sts for every 3 rows along right front edge, 43 (45, 47, 49, 51) [53, 55, 57, 59] sts along original CO edge, then 2 sts for every 3 rows down left front. Adjust, if needed, so there is an odd number of sts.

RIBBING SETUP ROW (WS): (P1, k1) repeat to last st, p1.

Cont in ribbing as est for 3 (3, 3.5, 3.5, 4)[4, 4.5, 4.5, 5]" / 7.5 (7.5, 9, 9, 10)[10, 11.5, 11.5, 12.5] cm.

Switch to larger circular needle.

Cont in ribbing as est for 3 (3, 3.5, 3.5, 4)[4, 4.5, 4.5, 5]" / 7.5 (7.5, 9, 9, 10)[10, 11.5, 11.5, 12.5] cm more.

BO loosely in ribbing.

Weave in all ends. Block to measurements.

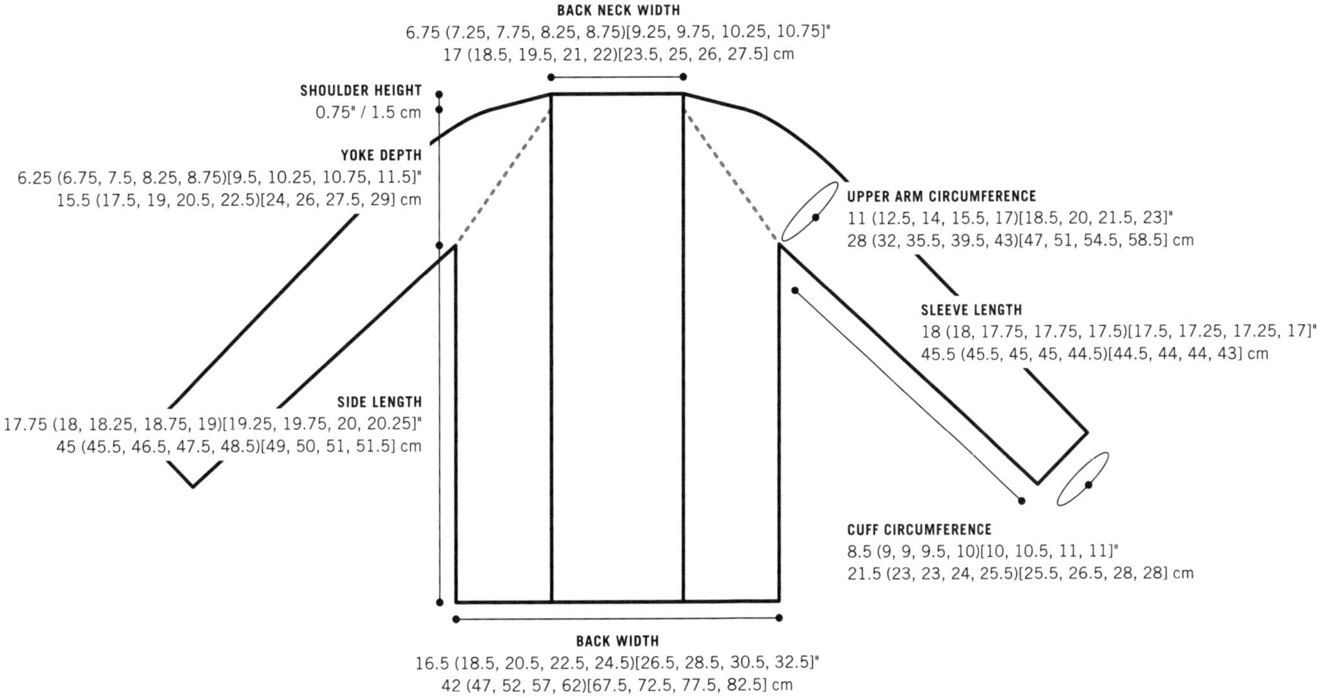

BACK NECK WIDTH
6.75 (7.25, 7.75, 8.25, 8.75)[9.25, 9.75, 10.25, 10.75]"
17 (18.5, 19.5, 21, 22)[23.5, 25, 26, 27.5] cm
SHOULDER HEIGHT
0.75" / 1.5 cm
YOKE DEPTH
6.25 (6.75, 7.5, 8.25, 8.75)[9.5, 10.25, 10.75, 11.5]"
15.5 (17.5, 19, 20.5, 22.5)[24, 26, 27.5, 29] cm
UPPER ARM CIRCUMFERENCE
11 (12.5, 14, 15.5, 17)[18.5, 20, 21.5, 23]"
28 (32, 35.5, 39.5, 43)[47, 51, 54.5, 58.5] cm
SLEEVE LENGTH
18 (18, 17.75, 17.75, 17.5)[17.5, 17.25, 17.25, 17]"
45.5 (45.5, 45, 45, 44.5)[44.5, 44, 44, 43] cm
SIDE LENGTH
17.75 (18, 18.25, 18.75, 19)[19.25, 19.75, 20, 20.25]"
45 (45.5, 46.5, 47.5, 48.5)[49, 50, 51, 51.5] cm
CUFF CIRCUMFERENCE
8.5 (9, 9, 9.5, 10)[10, 10.5, 11, 11]"
21.5 (23, 23, 24, 25.5)[25.5, 26.5, 28, 28] cm
BACK WIDTH
16.5 (18.5, 20.5, 22.5, 24.5)[26.5, 28.5, 30.5, 32.5]"
42 (47, 52, 57, 62)[67.5, 72.5, 77.5, 82.5] cm

SEAMING

Often knitters fall in one of two camps when it comes to seams: they either love them or avoid them whenever possible! While seams do require extra finishing, they serve a purpose that is worth considering.

Seams add structure to your knitwear. They hold the fabric in place, which helps the sweater hold its shape over time. Knitting in pieces also makes for more portable knitting: a top down seamless sweater can become quite cumbersome as it grows. This book features a nice mix of sweaters with seams and without. Even if it's outside your comfort zone, don't be afraid to try something different if the sweater construction is making a garment you'll enjoy wearing.

CREATE A NICE EDGE FOR SEAMING

To seam properly, you need a proper edge. This means we always work stitch patterns, increases and decreases at least one stitch in from the edge. Also, anywhere we're going to be picking up stitches, such as around the neck band to work a collar, we make sure there is an even, non-textured edge. If the garment is worked in an all-over stitch pattern, we simply knit the first row/round if it's top down, knit the last row / round if it's bottom up.

BLOCKING TEXTURED STITCHES

I like to steam block when I can: it's fast and easy. However, with textured knits steam blocking must be performed very carefully so as not to squish our beautiful three-dimensional textured stitches. Wet blocking is a good option for textured garments. Your gauge swatch is an excellent blocking guinea pig. Steam it, wet block it, see what it does and how you like the results. Then you can do the same for your finished garment.

HOW TO SET IN A SLEEVE

Step 1: Attach center of sleeve to shoulder seam with removable stitch marker.

Step 2: Using the working yarn threaded on a tapestry needle, begin attaching the horizontal edge of the top of the sleeve to the vertical edge of the armhole at a ratio of about 2 stitches for every 3 rows.

Step 3: Work in back and forth until you've worked 1" / 2.5 cm or so.

Step 4:. Pull yarn tight and admire your invisible seam!

Step 5: Continue until you reach the end of the horizontal top of the sleeve cap.

Steps 6 & 7: Line up sleeve cap and armhole edges to underarm edge and attach in a few spots using removable stitch markers.

Steps 8–10: Continue in Mattress Stitch to underarm edge.

Step 11: Attach horizontal underarm edges of sleeve cap and armhole.

Step 12: Continue in the same manner until you are back to shoulder seam. Weave in end on wrong side of fabric.

Admire!

WOOL SOAP
WITH LANOLIN

1
2
3
4
5
6
7
8
9
10
11
12

Enlarged texture

Top down button front cardigan

Modern classic

BULKY WEIGHT YARN

MORNING JACKET

MOSS STITCH PATTERN

worked flat over an odd number of sts

ROW 1 (RS): (P1, k1) repeat to last st, p1.
ROW 2 (WS): (K1, p1) repeat to last st, k1.
ROW 3: (K1, p1) repeat to last st, k1.
ROW 4: (P1, k1) repeat to last st, p1.

worked in the rnd over an even number of sts

RNDS 1 & 2: (K1, p1) repeat to end.
RNDS 3 & 4: (P1, k1) repeat to end.

ONE-ROW BUTTONHOLE

worked over 2 sts

With RS facing, move yarn to front, slip 1 st purlwise from left to right needle, then move yarn to back. * Slip the next st purlwise from left to right needle, then pass first slipped st over second slipped stitch; rep from * once more. 2 sts bound off. Slip st on right needle back to left needle. Turn work. With WS facing, CO 3 sts using knitted cast-on method. Turn work. With RS facing, slip 1 st purlwise from left to right needle. Pass last st cast on over slipped st. Slip 1 st purlwise from right needle back to left needle.

yoke

BEGIN AT THE TOP

Using circular needle and a long-tail cast on, CO 35 (35, 37, 37, 39)[39, 41, 41, 43] sts.

SETUP ROW (WS): P3, pm, p5, pm, p19 (19, 21, 21, 23)[23, 25, 25, 27], pm, p5, pm, p3.

ESTABLISH STITCH PATTERN

NEXT ROW (RS): K1, p1, k1, sm, (k1, work in Moss St to 1 st before marker, k1, sm) 3 times, k1, p1, k1.
NEXT ROW (WS): P1, k1, p1, sm, (p1, work in Moss St to 1 st before marker, p1, sm) 3 times, p1, k1, p1.

ROW 1—INC ROW (RS): K1, M1L, k1, M1R, k1, sm, (k1, M1L, work in Moss St to 1 st before marker, M1R, k1, sm) 3 times, k1, M1L, k1, M1R, k1. 10 sts inc.
ROW 2 (WS): (P1, work in Moss St to 1 st before marker, p1) 5 times, slipping markers as you come to them.
ROW 3—INC ROW: (K1, M1L, work in Moss St to 1 st before marker, M1R, k1) 5 times. 10 sts inc.
ROW 4: (P1, work in Moss St to 1 st before marker, p1) 5 times.

Rep Rows 3 & 4 twice more. 75 (75, 77, 77, 79)[79, 81, 81, 83] sts: 11 front sts, 13 sleeve sts, 27 (27, 29, 29, 31)[31, 33, 33, 35] back sts.

CAST ON STITCHES FOR FRONTS

INC ROW (RS): K1, (work as est to 1 st before m, M1R, k1, sm, k1, M1L) 4 times, work as est to end of row, then using a backward loop cast on, CO 6 (6, 7, 7, 8)[8, 9, 9, 10] sts.

finished measurements

Chest circumference: 33.5 (36.75, 40, 43.25, 46.5)[49.5, 52.75, 56, 59.25]" / 85.5 (93.5, 101.5, 109.5, 118) [126, 134, 142, 150.5] cm
Shown in size 33.5" / 85.5 cm with 0.5" / 1.5 cm of positive ease.

yarn

6 (7, 7, 8, 9)[9, 10, 11, 12] skeins Quince & Co. *Puffin* (100% American wool; 112 yd / 102 m per 100 g skein) in Egret

OR 600 (675, 750, 825, 900)[1000, 1075, 1175, 1250] yd / 550 (625, 675, 750, 825)[900, 975, 1050, 1150] m of bulky weight yarn

needles

US 15 / 10 mm:

- 24–32" / 60–80 cm circular needle
- set of double-pointed needles

Or size needed to obtain gauge.

notions

Stitch markers, stitch holders or waste yarn, tapestry needle, 7 (7, 7, 7, 8)[8, 8, 8, 9] buttons 1.375" / 35 mm diameter

gauge

10 sts and 16 rows = 4" / 10 cm in Moss Stitch pattern

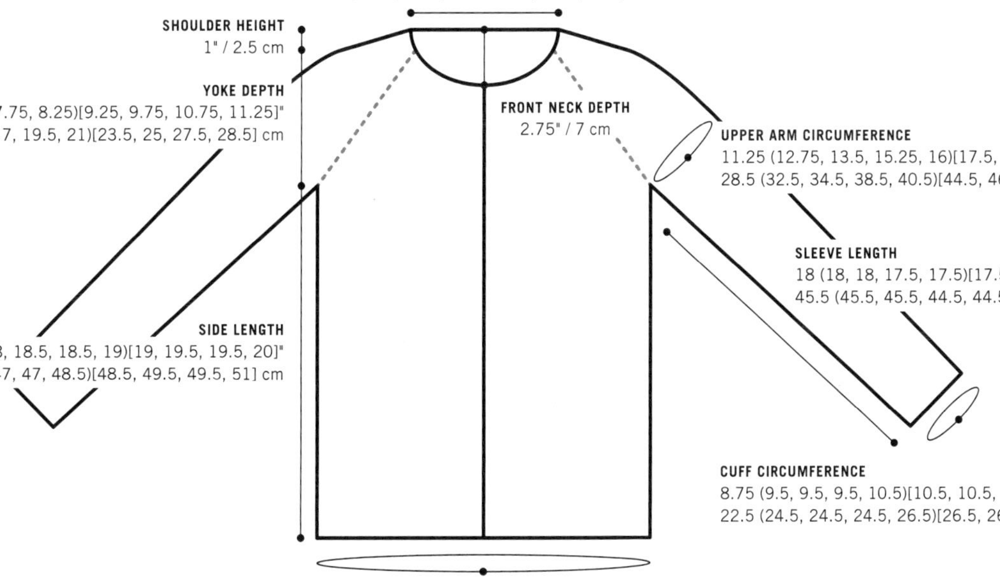

NEXT ROW (WS): (P1, work as est to 1 st before marker, p1) 5 times, then using a backward loop cast on, CO 6 (6, 7, 7, 8)[8, 9, 9, 10] sts. 93 (93, 97, 97, 101)[101, 105, 105, 109] sts: 18 (18, 19, 19, 20)[20, 21, 21, 22] front sts, 14 sleeve sts, 29 (29, 31, 31, 33)[33, 35, 35, 37] back sts.

ROW 1—INC ROW (RS): K6, (work as est to 1 st before m, M1R, k1, sm, k1, M1L) 4 times, work as est to last 6 sts, k6. 8 sts inc.
ROW 2 (WS): K6, work as est to last 6 sts, k6.

Rep this inc row 3 (5, 6, 8, 9)[11, 12, 14, 15] times more. 127 (143, 155, 171, 183)[199, 211, 227, 239] sts: 22 (24, 26, 28, 30)[32, 34, 36, 38] front sts, 23 (27, 29, 33, 35)[39, 41, 45, 47] sleeve sts, 37 (41, 45, 49, 53)[57, 61, 65, 69] back sts.

Work 3 (1, 1, 1, 1)[1, 1, 1, 1] row(s) even. Yoke meas approx 5.75 (6.25, 6.75, 7.75, 8.25)[9.25, 9.75, 10.75, 11.25]" / 14.5 (16, 17, 19.5, 21)[23.5, 25, 27.5, 28.5] cm.

AT THE SAME TIME, work buttonhole over the last 6 sts (the garter stitch band) on the RS row 4 rows from the top of the front cast on, then every 12 rows 6 (6, 6, 6, 7)[7, 7, 7, 8] times more as follows: K2, work One-Row Buttonhole over 2 sts, k2.

DIVIDE SLEEVES FROM BODY

NEXT ROW (RS): (Work as est to m, remove m, place 23 (27, 29, 33, 35)[39, 41, 45, 47] sleeve sts on a stitch holder, using a backward loop cast on, CO 5 sts) twice, work as est to end. 91 (99, 107, 115, 123)[131, 139, 147, 155] sts.

Cont as est, working body in Moss st and bands in garter st, until piece meas 13.5 (14, 14.5, 14.5, 15)[15, 15.5, 15.5, 16]" / 34.5 (35.5, 37, 37, 38)[38, 39.5, 39.5, 40.5] cm from underarm, ending with a RS row.

Work in garter st, knitting all rows for 4" / 10 cm, ending with a RS row. BO all sts knitwise.

sleeves

Divide 23 (27, 29, 33, 35)[39, 41, 45, 47] held sleeve sts evenly over 3 dpns. Using a 4th dpn pick up and knit first 3 sts of the 5 CO sts from the underarm, pm, pick up and knit last 2 sts, join for working in the rnd. 28 (30, 32, 38, 40)[44, 46, 50, 52] sts.

Work in Moss st as est for 14 (10, 10, 6, 6)[5, 4, 4, 3] rnds.

DEC RND: Ssk, work to last 2 sts, k2tog. 2 sts dec.

Rep this dec rnd every 15 (11, 11, 7, 7)[6, 5, 5, 4] rnds 2 (3, 1, 6, 6)[4, 7, 3, 11] time(s) more, then every - (-, 10, -, -)[5, 4, 4, -) rnds 0 (0, 3, 0, 0)[4, 2, 7, 0] times more. 22 (24, 24, 24, 26)[26, 26, 28, 28] sts.

Cont as est until sleeve meas 14 (14, 14, 13.5, 13.5)[13.5, 13, 13, 13]" / 35.5 (35.5, 35.5, 34.5, 34.5)[34.5, 33, 33, 33] cm, or 4" / 10 cm shorter than desired length, ending with Rnd 1 or 3 of Moss St.

Beg with a purl rnd, work in garter st for 4" / 10 cm, ending with a knit rnd.

BO all sts purlwise.

finishing

COLLAR

With RS facing and starting at right front, pick up and knit 6 (6, 7, 7, 8)[8, 9, 9, 10] sts along top of band, 6 sts along right neck edge, 33 (33, 35, 35, 37)[37, 39, 39, 41] sts along CO edge, 6 sts along left front neck, then 6 (6, 7, 7, 8)[8, 9, 9, 10] sts along top of left band. 55 (55, 59, 59, 63)[63, 67, 67, 71] sts.

Work in garter st, knitting all rows for 2" / 5 cm, ending with a RS row. BO all sts knitwise.

Weave in all ends. Block to measurements.

Sew buttons to band opposite buttonholes.

Big texture

Statement accessories

BULKY WEIGHT YARN

Plaid and striped tops: LL Bean Signature

COWLS

big texture cowl

Using smaller circular needle and a long-tail cast on, CO 88 sts. Join for working in the rnd, being careful to not twist sts. Pm to mark beg of the rnd.

RIBBING SETUP RND: (K1, p1) repeat to end.

Cont in ribbing as est for 3 rnds more.

Switch to larger circular needle.

BEGIN MOSS STITCH PATTERN

RNDS 1 & 2: (K1, p1) repeat to end.
RNDS 3 & 4: (P1, k1) repeat to end.

Cont as est until cowl meas 9" / 23 cm, or 1" / 2.5 cm shorter than desired length.

Work in ribbing for 4 rnds.

BO loosely in ribbing.

finishing

Weave in all ends. Block to measurements.

finished measurements

Circumference: 35.25" / 89.5 cm
Height: 10" / 25.5 cm

yarn

2 skeins Quince & Co. *Puffin* (100% American wool; 112 yd / 102 m per 100 g skein) in Glacier

OR 175 yd / 150 m of bulky weight yarn

needles

US 15 / 10 mm:

- 24–32" / 60–80 cm circular needle

US 13 / 9 mm:

- 24–32" / 60–80 cm circular needle

Or size needed to obtain gauge.

notions

Stitch marker, tapestry needle

gauge

10 sts and 16 rnds = 4" / 10 cm in Moss Stitch pattern using larger needles

big cable cowl

Using smaller circular needle and a long-tail cast on, CO 180 sts. Join for working in the rnd, being careful to not twist sts. Pm to mark beg of the rnd.

RIBBING SETUP RND: (K1, p1) repeat to end.

Cont in ribbing as est for 5 rnds more.

Switch to larger circular needle.

BEGIN HORSESHOE CABLE STITCH PATTERN

RNDS 1–4: Knit.
RND 5: (C6B, C6F) repeat to end.
RNDS 6–8: Knit.

Rep these 8 rnds 5 times more.

DEC RND: (K2, k2tog) repeat to end. 135 sts.

Switch to smaller circular needle.

Work in ribbing for 6 rnds.

BO all sts in ribbing.

finishing

Weave in all ends.

Block to measurements.

finished measurements

Circumference: 36" / 91.5 cm
Height: 10.75" / 27 cm

yarn

2 skeins Quince & Co. *Osprey* (100% American wool; 170 yd / 155 m per 100 g skein) in Shell

OR 325 yd / 300 m of aran weight yarn

needles

US 10.5 / 6.5 mm:

- 24–32" / 60–80 cm circular needle

US 9 / 5.5 mm:

- 24–32" / 60–80 cm circular needle

Or size needed to obtain gauge.

notions

Stitch marker, cable needle, tapestry needle

gauge

20 sts and 22 rnds = 4" / 10 cm in Horseshoe Cable Stitch pattern using larger needles; 1 cable pattern repeat (12 sts and 8 rnds) = 2.25" / 6 cm wide and 1.5" / 4 cm tall

TECHNIQUES

VIDEO TUTORIALS available at knitbot.com for:

Backward loop cast on, Long tail cast on, Tubular cast on

The internet is an excellent teaching resource. Search and find video tutorials for **Mattress Stitch, Kitchener Stitch, Three-needle bind-off** and **Knitted Cast On**.

Learn all kinds of helpful tips and techniques in my online class:

www.knitbot.com/knit-stars

INCREASES

M1L (make 1 left slanting): Insert left-hand needle from front to back under horizontal strand between stitch just worked and next stitch, knit lifted strand through the back loop (1 stitch increased).

M1R (make 1 right slanting): Insert left-hand needle from back to front under horizontal strand between stitch just worked and next stitch, knit lifted strand through the front loop (1 stitch increased).

DECREASES

k2tog: Knit 2 stitches together (1 stitch decreased, leans to the right).

ssk (slip, slip, knit): Slip 2 stitches one at a time knitwise to the right hand needle; return stitches to left-hand needle in turned position and knit them together through the back loops (1 stitch decreased, leans to the left).

ABBREVIATIONS

CABLES

C4B: Slip 2 stitches to cable needle and hold at back, knit next 2 stitches from the left-hand needle, then knit 2 stitches from the cable needle.

C4F: Slip 2 stitches to cable needle and hold at front, knit next 2 stitches from the left-hand needle, then knit 2 stitches from the cable needle.

C6B: Slip 3 stitches to cable needle and hold at back, knit next 3 stitches from the left-hand needle, then knit 3 stitches from the cable needle.

C6F: Slip 3 stitches to cable needle and hold at front, knit next 3 stitches from the left-hand needle, then knit 3 stitches from the cable needle.

C8B: Slip 4 stitches to cable needle and hold at back, knit next 4 stitches from the left-hand needle, then knit 4 stitches from the cable needle.

C8F: Slip 4 stitches to cable needle and hold at front, knit next 4 stitches from the left-hand needle, then knit 4 stitches from the cable needle.

approx: approximately

beg: beginning

BO: bind off

CO: cast on

cont: continue(s)(ing)

dec: decrease(d)(s)(ing)

dpn(s): double-pointed needle(s)

EOR: every other row / round

est: established

garter stitch: Knit all rows when working flat. Alternate knit 1 round, purl 1 round when working in the round.

inc: increase(d)(s)(ing)

k: knit

k2tog: knit two stitches together

k3tog: knit three stitches together

m: marker

M1L: make 1 left increase. See Techniques.

M1R: make 1 right increase. See Techniques.

meas: measure(s)(ing)

p: purl

p2tog: purl two stitches together

patt(s): pattern(s)

pm: place marker

rem(s): remain(s)(ing)

rep(s): repeat(s)

RS: Right Side

sm: slip marker

ssk: slip, slip, knit

St st: Stockinette stitch. Knit on the right side, purl on the wrong side. When working in the round, knit all rounds.

st(s): stitch(es)

WS: Wrong Side

ACKNOWLEDGMENTS

A special thank you to Ryan FitzGerald for giving me the opportunity to publish this book and Pam Allen for all the knowledge she has shared with me.

Thank you to The Portland Regency Hotel & Spa for giving us a space to work in during this project, and to Eventide Oyster Company for letting us shoot in their beautiful space!

Photography: Whitney Hayward
Graphic Design: Mary Joy Gumayagay
Technical Edit: Tana Pageler

Models: Jennie Ross, Eric Lindgren
Hair and Makeup: Amy Valente
Wardrobe: More & Co., LL Bean, Bliss Boutiques
Tools: Twig & Horn

Team Quince: Leila Raabe, Jerusha Robinson,
Dawn Catanzaro, Adi Kehoe